GUITAR: TOTAL SCALES TECHNIQUES AND APPLICATIONS
(TSTA)

2008 Revised & Updated

CREATED AND WRITTEN BY MARK JOHN STERNAL

MJS MUSIC & ENTERTAINMENT, LLC.
www.MJSPublications.com

For distribution contact:
MJS Music & Entertainment, LLC
9699 W. Fort Island Trail
Crystal River, FL 34429
352-563-1779

Dealer Inquiries Welcome

Written and arranged by Mark Sternal
Edited by Mark & Jeanne Sternal

Cover, Photos and Concept by Mark & Jeanne Sternal
Back cover industry and magazine quotations are for the Total Scales Techniques and Applications series.

Licensed by Gibson: "The body shapes of the Gibson J-150 Super Jumbo Acoustic and Gibson Les Paul Standard guitars are registered trademarks of Gibson Guitar Corp., Nashville, TN."

ISBN 978-0-9762917-0-1

TABLE OF CONTENTS

INTRODUCTION

Although I am a guitar teacher, I still consider myself a student. For most of my life I have studied the guitar. I am constantly learning new techniques, applications, and combinations. I have studied under a number of great guitarists and musicians both privately and in the classroom, throughout high school, college and my adult life. My occupation includes teaching, writing, live performances, and studio recordings.

My purpose for writing this book is to teach all that I have learned in a fraction of the time it has taken me to learn it. The students I have personally taught range in age from 5 through 86. I've never turned down a student because of lack of talent. I have developed a method of teaching which will take a person from a complete beginner to a professional level, playing and understanding every note on the guitar. My method of teaching is offered in this book. It has taken over 20 years to acquire this knowledge and develop my method.

The first chapter of this book will be a comprehensive look at the fundamentals of the guitar. I am of strong belief that musicians should know their instruments, and you as a guitarist should know your guitar.

The following chapters, for the most part, will be pure playing. You will learn to play scales and use them musically on the entire fretboard. We will concentrate on speed, accuracy, ear training, and creativity. Throughout this course we will add new tricks, techniques, patterns and applications to every note and every scale position.

When you have finished this course, you will have at your command an unlimited musical vocabulary for your guitar.

Have fun, and be creative. Study the material in this book for at least 15 minutes a day in addition to your current practice time. Work hard and it will come easy.

Mark John Sternal

E-mail Support

I'm always happy to help with any questions you have regarding any lesson in this book. If you follow each lesson page by page you shouldn't have a problem understanding the music and text. If, however, you ever run into a problem please send me an e-mail at msternal@mjspublications.com.

TAB or Tablature Explanation

Tablature or Tab is sometimes referred to as the 6 line staff, or the guitar staff. Each line represents a string. The bottom line being the 6th and lowest pitch string (the thickest string), and the top line representing the 1st or highest pitch string (the thinnest string).

Instead of using musical notes for each line, numbers are used to represent the frets that are to be played.

EXAMPLE 1: If a 4 is written on the 3rd line, you would play the 4th fret on the 3rd string.

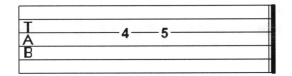

EXAMPLE 2: If a 4 is written on the 3rd line followed by a 5, you would play the 4th fret on the 3rd string (**ex. 1**), followed by the 5th fret on the 3rd string (**ex. 2**).

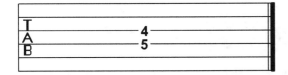

EXAMPLE 3: If you are to play more than one note at a time, the notes would be written one on top of the other. If a 4 is written on the 3rd line, and directly below it a 5 is written on the 4th line, you would play the 4th fret on the 3rd string, along with the 5th fret on the 4th string at the same time.

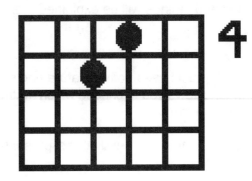

Music Notation

Notes on the Staff
The staff notes of the treble clef start with E on the very bottom line. The space above E represents an F note. The line above F represents a G.

E   F   G   A   B   C   D   E   F

Ledger Lines
Notes can extend above and below the staff by the use of ledger lines.

F   G   A   B   C   D   G   A   B   C   D   E

COMMON SYMBOLS

BAR LINES: the vertical lines that divide tablature and staff music into sections, (***B.L.*** in example below).

MEASURE: the space between bar lines.

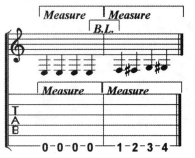

TIMING: Music is defined as the study of time and sound. Notice that in this definition the word time comes before sound. Timing is the most important part of music. Anyone can make noise/sound, but when you apply sound to a rhythm pattern or timing, you make music.

There are many different timings in music. Some of the most common timings are:

3/4 timing = 3 beats per measure
4/4 timing = 4 beats per measure
2/4 timing = 2 beats per measure

There are many different timing notes. Some of the common timing notes used on the guitar are: The whole note = 4 beats each. Half note = 2 beats each. Quarter note = 1 beat each. Eighth note = ½ beat each. Sixteenth note = 1/4 beat each.

Whole	Half	Quarter	Eighth	Sixteenth
4 beats	2 beats	1 beat	1/2 beat	1/4 beat

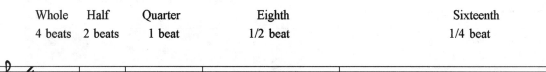

These notes and timings will be explained more thoroughly as they are used throughout this course.

TAB/STAFF

Popular guitar music uses both tablature and staff notation which allows you to choose which method of reading you prefer.

The exercises in this book will all be presented using TAB/STAFF.

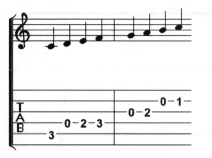

CHAPTER 1

PART 1. THE MUSICAL ALPHABET

The musical alphabet consists of 12 notes.

A	A#/Bb	B	C	C#/Db	D	D#/Eb	E	F	F#/Gb	G	G#/Ab	A
1	2	3	4	5	6	7	8	9	10	11	12	1

*Notice that the 2nd, 5th, 7th, 10th, and 12th notes have 2 different names. For example, the 2nd note can be an A#(A sharp) or a Bb(B flat). It is the same note but it has two different names.

The notes **A, B, C, D, E, F, & G** are called basic or natural notes.

The notes **A#/Bb, C#/Db, D#/Eb, F#/Gb, & G#/Ab** are called accidentals. Accidental notes will be used later on in this study course.

PART 2. THE MUSICAL ALPHABET AND THE GUITAR

Each of the six strings of the guitar have been assigned a specific note. The 6th string, which is the top and heaviest string is an E note. It is called the low E string. When this string is played OPEN (no frets), it will produce an E pitch. Each fret after that will bring you to the next note in the musical alphabet.

EXAMPLE. If you play the 1st fret of the 6th string it will produce a F note, the 2nd fret will produce a F#/Gb note, 3rd fret will produce a G note, next a G#/Ab note, then A, the 6th fret will be an A#/Bb note, 7th fret B, 8th C, ETC... Once you reach the 12th fret the musical alphabet will repeat itself starting with the E note.

The 5th string open is an A note.
The 4th string is a D note.
3rd string is a G note.
2nd is the B string.
The 1st string is the high E string.

Below is a note chart provided for the readers reference.

	6th String	5th String	4th String	3rd String	2nd String	1st String	
OPEN	E	A	D	G	B	E	OPEN
1ST	F	A#/Bb	D#/Eb	G#/Ab	C	F	1ST
2ND	F#/Gb	B	E	A	C#/Db	F#/Gb	2ND
3RD	G	C	F	A#/Bb	D	G	3RD
4TH	G#/Ab	C#/Db	F#/Gb	B	D#/Eb	G#/Ab	4TH
5TH	A	D	G	C	E	A	5TH
6TH	A#/Bb	D#/Eb	G#/Ab	C#/Db	F	A#/Bb	6TH
7TH	B	E	A	D	F#/Gb	B	7TH
8TH	C	F	A#/Bb	D#/Eb	G	C	8TH
9TH	C#/Db	F#/Gb	B	E	G#/Ab	C#/Db	9TH
10TH	D	G	C	F	A	D	10TH
11TH	D#/Eb	G#/Ab	C#/Db	F#/Gb	A#/Bb	D#/Eb	11TH
12TH	E	A	D	G	B	E	12TH
13TH	F	A#/Bb	D#/Eb	G#/Ab	C	F	13TH
14TH	F#/Gb	B	E	A	C#/Db	F#/Gb	14TH
15TH	G	C	F	A#/Bb	D	G	15TH
16TH	G#/Ab	C#/Db	F#/Gb	B	D#/Eb	G#/Ab	16TH
17TH	A	D	G	C	E	A	17TH
18TH	A#/Bb	D#/Eb	G#/Ab	C#/Db	F	A#/Bb	18TH
19TH	B	E	A	D	F#/Gb	B	19TH
20TH	C	F	A#/Bb	D#/Eb	G	C	20TH
21ST	C#/Db	F#/Gb	B	E	G#/Ab	C#/Db	21ST
22ND	D	G	C	F	A	D	22ND
23RD	D#/Eb	G#/Ab	C#/Db	F#/Gb	A#/Bb	D#/Eb	23RD
24TH	E	A	D	G	B	E	24TH

PART 3. **TUNING**

Some notes have been highlighted and are connected by a line. The notes that share the same color highlight are the same pitch and will aid you in tuning your guitar.

EXAMPLE. If your low E string is in tune, you can use the **A** note on the 5th fret/6th string to tune the open **A** note on the 5th string. Play the 5th fret of the low E string, then play the open A string, compare the 2 notes, and adjust the pitch of the 5th string to match that of the 6th string/5th fret by tightening or loosening the tuning peg.

You can apply this to the 5th fret of the 5th string to tune the 4th string to a **D** note.

Then the 5th fret of the 4th string to tune the 3rd string to a **G** note.

The **4th** fret of the 3rd string to tune the 2nd string to a **B** note.

And the 5th fret of the 2nd string to tune the 1st string to an **E** note.

If you're having a hard time tuning your guitar, I recommend an electric tuner. Electric tuners are inexpensive and will save you from the frustration that comes with playing a guitar that is out of tune.

If your guitar goes out of tune easily, or if it sounds out of tune when you play the higher numbered frets take it to your local music store and have a guitar technician take a look at it, chances are it may only need a few minor adjustments.

CHAPTER 2

THE NATURAL SCALE
A,B,C,D,E,F,G,A,B,C,D,E,F,G,A,B,C,D,E,F,G,A,B,C,D,E,F,G,A,B,C,D,E,F,GA,B,C,D,E,F,G

Most of the material in this book will be taught using the natural scale. A,B,C,D,E,F,G,A
 It is called the natural scale because it consists of all the natural notes and no accidentals (sharps # or flats b).

Scales are the key to writing music. The notes of a scale compliment each other, and can be used together to create chords, melodies, and harmonies, giving you a solid foundation to build or write your own songs, as well as learn your favorite pieces from other musicians.

PART 1. MAJOR AND MINOR ROOT NOTES
The two most common types of scales are the major and minor scales. A major scale has what some would describe as a bright or happy sound. A minor scale has what someone might describe as a mellow, soft or sad sound. The natural scale, ABCDEFG, consists of both the major and minor scales within its notes.

To determine whether or not a scale is major or minor, in this case, would depend on what we call the 'root note'.

The root note is the main note of a song/scale.

For Example: When using the natural scale, if our root note is a C note, C D E F G A B C, our scale is major. If our root note is an A note, A B C D E F G A, our scale is minor. Throughout this book we will pay close attention to our minor and major root notes. Minor root notes will be referred to with a small case "m". So the note "A minor" will be referred to as **Am**. Major root notes will be referred to with a ^ symbol. So C major will be **C^**.

Knowing the locations of your root notes will give you the ability to write a song in the major or minor key and/or change any song from major to minor, in any scale position. This will also allow you to change keys during a song.

There are 7 notes in the natural scale, | 1 2 3 4 5 6 7 |, therefore we have 7 scale positions. Each of | A B C D E F G |

the 7 scale positions start with a different note of the natural scale. In each position we will play 3 scale notes per string on all 6 strings.

CHAPTER 3

FINGER AND HAND POSITIONING

Positioning of your right and left hand is very important when playing the guitar. Pay close attention to this chapter, and get in the habit of keeping your fingers and hands in the proper positions at all times. This will allow you to achieve desirable results quicker.

Throughout this book we will refer to your index finger as I or your 1st finger, your middle finger as m or your 2nd finger, your ring finger as r or your 3rd finger, and your pinkie as p or your 4th finger.

PART 1. YOUR PICKING HAND

Hold your pick between your thumb and your index finger. The tip of the pick should be pointing in the direction of your index finger.

Always alternate your picking strokes. Down, up, down, up. Bend your wrist or your elbow when picking. Avoid any movement of your thumb or index finger. Your other three fingers should be rolled into your palm or stretched out and braced against the body of your guitar below the first string.

Down Stroke Symbol	Up Stroke Symbol	Always Alternate Your Picking Strokes
⊓ ⊓ ⊓ ⊓	v v v v	⊓ v ⊓ v ⊓ v ⊓ v ⊓ v

If you are a beginner guitarist or if this is a new technique for you, take some time to practice it. The following exercises will help you develop this technique.

OPEN SIX STRING EXERCISE

1. This exercise is written in 4/4 timing using quarter notes. There are 4 beats per measure. A quarter note receives one beat. The count, is 1-2-3-4/1-2-3-4, (the count is written below the piece of music indicated by a "C"). Use alternate picking strokes.

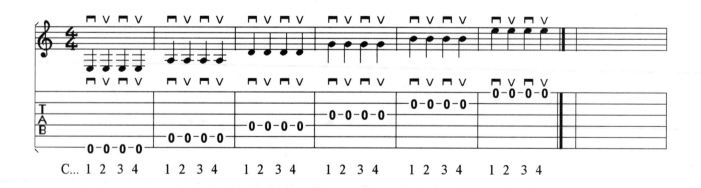

2. This exercise is written in 3/4 timing using quarter notes. There are 3 beats per measure. A quarter note receives one beat. The count is 1-2-3/1-2-3.

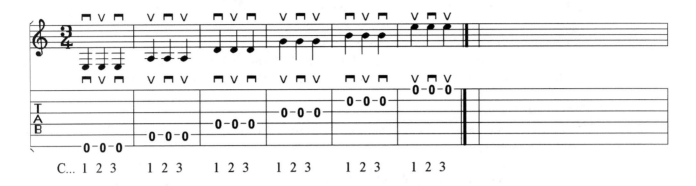

3. This exercise is written in 3/4 timing using eighth notes. There are 3 beats per measure. An eighth note receives half a beat. The count is 1-&-2-&-3-&/1-&-2-&-3-&.

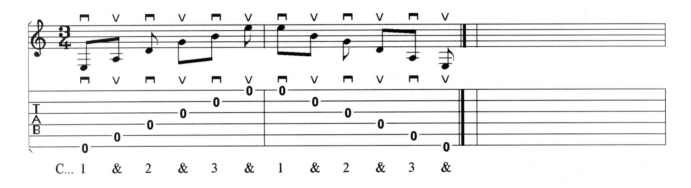

PART 2. THE PLAYING HAND

Position the fingers of your playing hand one fret apart each.

Ex. On the 6th string, press down on the 1st fret with your first finger.

2nd fret, 2nd finger.

3rd fret, 3rd finger.

And 4th fret, 4th finger.

Keep your thumb behind your middle finger in the center of the neck. Many guitarists allow their thumb to hang over the top edge of the guitar. There are some techniques that require this positioning but overall it will slow you down when playing scales. When you are not playing a note your fingers should remain in this position, one half inch above the string. Always keep your thumb in contact with the neck of your guitar. **This positioning should be used anywhere on the fretboard.**

Read this section again and again until proper positioning of your hands become second nature. Get in the habit of checking your positioning every time you play your guitar. **THIS IS VERY IMPORTANT!**

CHAPTER 4
PLAYING THE NATURAL SCALE
As mentioned earlier, there are 7 notes in the natural scale, therefore we have 7 scale positions.

1	2	3	4	5	6	7
C	D	E	F	G	A	B

Each position starts with a different scale note. The beauty of these 7 positions is that they are universal for every key of music. So later on when we start learning key changes, you will already know the finger patterns.

TO MEMORIZE OR NOT?
While it is important to know these scales, you may move on without memorizing them. As long as you are comfortable playing them, and you are using the proper fingerings, keep moving through this course. These positions will be re-introduced time and time again using different tricks, techniques and applications. By the time you get half way through this book, you will probably have the positions memorized from playing them musically.

E POSITION C major / Am SCALE or Third Position

Since E is the lowest possible note on a standard tuned guitar, we are going to begin our scale patterns on the E note. In the key of C major, E is the third note.

C   D   E
1   2   3

so the E position is also known as the 3rd position.

^ = Major Root
m = minor root

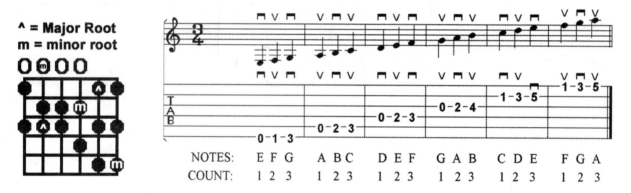

C^ root notes are on the 5th string - 3rd fret, and 2nd string - 1st fret.
Am root notes are on the 5th string - open, 3rd string - 2nd fret, and 1st string - 5th fret.

Step By Step Break Down:
      Lets begin with a step by step approach to playing our scale. What we want to accomplish here is proper fingering and picking techniques. First, slowly go through the scale, making sure to use the correct fingers and picking techniques. Once you get comfortable playing the scale, speed up your tempo.

FIRST MEASURE 6th String Notes
  1. E Note. First we begin with a downstroke of the pick on the open 6 string for the 1 count.
  2. F Note. Next we will play an up-stroke of the pick on the 1st fret, 1st finger, sixth string for the 2 count.
  3. G Note. Then a downstroke on the 3rd fret, 3rd finger for the 3 count. When picking the 3rd fret of the 6th string, you also want to bring the pick down over the 5th string, without picking it, all in one movement.
SECOND MEASURE 5th String Notes
  1. A Note. Play the 5th string open with an up-stroke for the 1st count.
  2. B Note. Downstroke on the 2nd fret, 2nd finger for the 2nd count.
  3. C Note. Up-stroke on the 3rd fret, 3rd finger for the 3rd count.

APPLY THIS ALTERNATE PICKING TECHNIQUE TO ALL OF YOUR GUITAR PLAYING.

Allow each note to ring out until the next note is played. FOR EXAMPLE: On the sixth string when you are playing the 1st fret, hold that note until you have played the 3rd fret, <u>then</u> lift the first finger from the 1st fret.

THIRD MEASURE   4th String Notes
1. D Note. Downstroke on the open 4th string for the 1st count.
2. E Note. Up-stroke on the 2nd finger, 2nd fret for the 2nd count.
3. F Note. Downstroke on the 3rd finger, 3rd fret for the 3rd count.

FOURTH MEASURE   3rd String Notes
1. G Note. Up-stroke on the open 3rd string, 1st count.
2. A Note. Downstroke on the 2nd fret, 2nd finger, 2nd count.
3. B Note. Up-stroke on the 4th fret, 4th finger, 3rd count.

The 2nd & 1st string notes require a stretch which may require some practice for beginner guitarists.

FIFTH MEASURE   2nd String Notes
1. C Note. Downstroke, 1st fret, 1st finger, 1st count.
2. D Note. Up-stroke, 3rd fret, 2nd finger, 2nd count.
3. E Note. Downstroke, 5th fret, 4th finger, 3rd count

SIXTH MEASURE   1st String Notes
1. F Note. Up-stroke, 1st fret, 1st finger, 1st count.
2. G Note. Downstroke, 3rd fret, 2nd finger, 2nd count.
3. A Note. Up-stroke, 5th fret, 4th finger, 3rd count.

Remember to keep the thumb of your playing hand directly behind your middle finger, in the center of the neck. For the scale position we just learned, your thumb should be behind the 2nd fret for the 6th, 5th, 4th, & 3rd strings, then slide it up behind the 3rd fret for the 2nd & 1st string.

Learning Tips For Beginners
An entire piece of sheet music can sometimes look menacing. Break it down into small sections that you can handle. For example, focus on the first measure, play it, then play it again. In fact, loop it over and over until it becomes smooth. Now learn the second measure by itself. When it becomes comfortable, combine the two measures. Keep adding measure by measure, and pretty soon you'll be playing entire musical pieces in one sitting.

F POSITION C^/Am SCALE
or Fourth Position

F is the 4th note in the C^ scale so it is also called as the 4th position C^ scale.

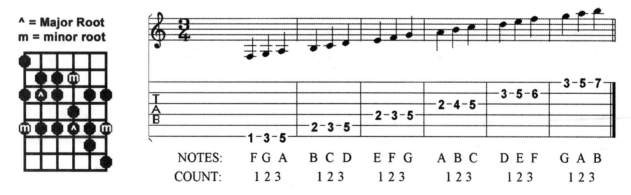

C^ root notes are on the 5th string - 3rd fret, and 3rd string - 5th fret.
Am root notes are on the 6th string - 5th fret, 3rd string - 2nd fret, and 1st string 5th fret.

Step By Step Break Down:

For the F position your thumb should be behind the 3rd fret for the top 4 strings, then slide it up behind the 5th fret for the 2nd & 1st string.

Use fingers 1, 2, & 4 for the 6th, 5th, & 4th strings. Use fingers 1, 3, & 4 for the 3rd, & 2nd string. And back to fingers 1, 2, & 4 for the 1st string.

Remember, allow each note to ring out until the next one is played. Also, always use alternate picking.

Tips For Increasing Speed

Play along with a metronome starting at a slow pace. When you can repeat a section a few times without error, increase the tempo 3 to 5 notches. If you can still play it comfortably at that pace, increase the tempo more. Do this until you reach your breaking point and make a note of the tempo. If your top speed is 100 beats per minute, try for 105 the next day, then 110 the day after. Keep doing this and you'll be playing lightning fast in no time.

G or 5TH POSITION C^/Am SCALE

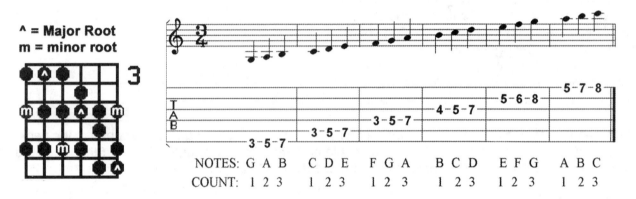

^ = Major Root
m = minor root

NOTES:	G A B	C D E	F G A	B C D	E F G	A B C
COUNT:	1 2 3	1 2 3	1 2 3	1 2 3	1 2 3	1 2 3

C^ root notes are on the 5th string - 3rd fret, 3rd string - 5th fret, and 1st string - 8th fret.
Am root notes are on the 6th string - 5th fret, 4th string - 7th fret, and 1st string 5th fret.

Step By Step Break Down:

Use your 1st, 2nd, & 4th fingers for the top 5 strings, and your 1st, 3rd & 4th fingers for the 1st string.

Place your thumb behind the 5th fret for the top 4 strings then slide it up behind the 6th fret for the 2nd & 1st strings.

A OR 6TH POSITION C^/Am SCALE.
A IS ALSO THE ROOT OR 1ST POSITION MINOR SCALE.

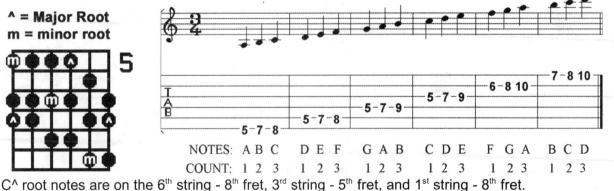

^ = Major Root
m = minor root

NOTES:	A B C	D E F	G A B	C D E	F G A	B C D
COUNT:	1 2 3	1 2 3	1 2 3	1 2 3	1 2 3	1 2 3

C^ root notes are on the 6th string - 8th fret, 3rd string - 5th fret, and 1st string - 8th fret.
Am root notes are on the 6th string - 5th fret, 4th string - 7th fret, and 2nd string - 10th fret.

Step By Step Break Down:
   Place your thumb behind the 6th/7th fret for the top 4 strings, 8th fret for the 1st & 2nd strings.
   Use fingers 1, 3, & 4 for the 6th and 5th strings, and fingers 1, 2, & 4 for the remaining 4 strings.
   Remember, allow each note to ring out until the next one is played.

B OR 7TH POSITION C^/Am SCALE

^ = Major Root
m = minor root

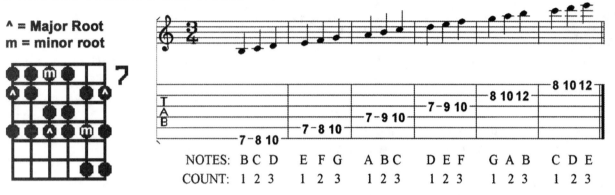

NOTES:	B C D	E F G	A B C	D E F	G A B	C D E
COUNT:	1 2 3	1 2 3	1 2 3	1 2 3	1 2 3	1 2 3

C^ root notes are on the 6th string - 8th fret, 4th string - 10th fret, and 1st string - 8th fret.
Am root notes are on the 4th string - 7th fret, and 2nd string - 10th fret.

Step By Step Break Down:
   Thumb behind the 8th fret for the top 4 strings, 10th fret for the 2nd & 1st strings.
   Fingers 1, 2, & 4 for the 6th & 5th strings, fingers 1, 3, & 4 for the 4th & 3rd strings, and 1, 2, & 4 for the 2nd & 1st string.

C OR 1ST POSITION C^/Am SCALE

^ = Major Root
m = minor root

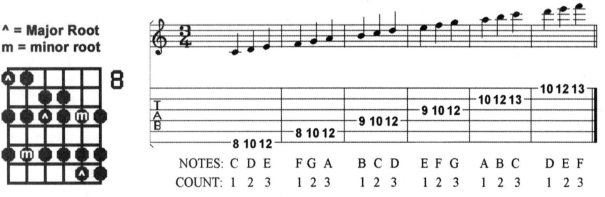

NOTES:	C D E	F G A	B C D	E F G	A B C	D E F
COUNT:	1 2 3	1 2 3	1 2 3	1 2 3	1 2 3	1 2 3

C^ root notes are on the 6th string - 8th fret, 4th string - 10th fret, and 2nd string - 13th fret.
Am root notes are on the 5th string 12th fret, and 2nd string - 10th fret.

Step By Step Break Down:
   Thumb behind the 10th fret for the top 4 strings, 12th fret for the 2nd & 1st strings.
   Fingers 1, 2, & 4 for the top 4 strings, and 1, 3, & 4 for the rest.

D OR 2ND POSITION C^/Am

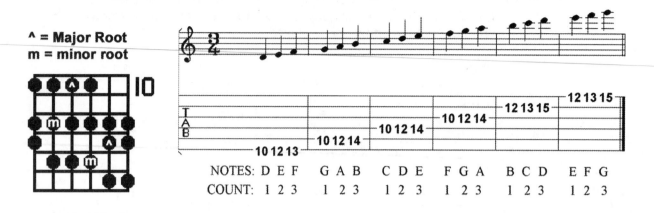

^ = Major Root
m = minor root

NOTES:	D E F	G A B	C D E	F G A	B C D	E F G
COUNT:	1 2 3	1 2 3	1 2 3	1 2 3	1 2 3	1 2 3

C^ root notes are on the 4th string - 10th fret, and 2nd string - 13th fret.
Am root notes are on the 5th string 12th fret, and 3rd string - 14th fret.

Step By Step Break Down:

Thumb behind 11th/12th fret for top 4 strings, 13th for the rest.
Fingers 1, 3, & 4 for the 6th string, and fingers 1, 2, & 4 for the rest.

E OCTAVE or 3RD POSITION C^/Am SCALE

Here's the E OR 3RD POSITION again. This is the OCTAVE OF OPEN POSITION

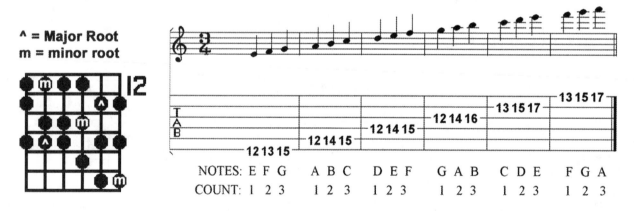

^ = Major Root
m = minor root

NOTES:	E F G	A B C	D E F	G A B	C D E	F G A
COUNT:	1 2 3	1 2 3	1 2 3	1 2 3	1 2 3	1 2 3

C^ root notes are on the 5th string - 15th fret, and 2nd string - 13th fret.
Am root notes are on the 5th string 12th fret, 3rd string - 14th fret, and 1st string 17th fret.

Notice that the notes in this position are patterned identically to the notes of the open position. It is the same position played one octave, or 12 notes/frets higher. This can be applied to every position. F starting with the 13th fret of the 6th string. G with the 15th, A with the 17th, B w/19th, C w/20th & D w/22nd provided that your guitar's frets go high enough.

INTRO TO SOLOING

People often ask me "how do you write guitar solos?" The answer can be both simple and complex. I'll start out by answering simply, and throughout this course, I'll give you ideas for making your leads and solo's more complex.

Scale notes compliment each other. Use these notes together to create music. To start, use scale notes only. Try any combination of scale notes. If you are playing with another musician, he or she should use chords taken from the scale you are playing. **FOR EXAMPLE:** C, F & G are scale notes that can be used as chords. If the other musician is playing a rhythm using these chords, you can play the natural scale along with the chords for a lead or solo. To make your solos stand out, you can use the different techniques and applications provided in this book, and even invent a few of your own. As you get more comfortable with soloing, you can begin to change keys, and even scales during a solo, lead, or song.

There is no end to the possibilities of what you can do to any single note. Take this scale and explore every possibility. Music is emotion. Learn to put your personal feelings into your playing. Happiness, sadness, love, hate, excitement, aggression, etc... These are your personal feelings that you can express in your music. Write them, learn them, play them fast and slow.

Question And Answer Soloing

Q & A soloing is another technique used for creating leads. Pick a scale. By playing any combination of scale notes, other than the root note (key note), you can write a melody that sounds incomplete. This will pose as a question. To complete the question, play any combination of scale notes, ending on the root note. This will pose as an answer.

Example:
Take our scale which is in the key of Am.
For the question, play C, D then E.
For the answer, play D, C, end on A.

Another way to play a question phrase is to play any combination of scale notes, <u>including</u> the root note, but not ending on the root note.
Example: A, C, D, C/ A, C, D, D.

You can also play different combinations of Q & A phrases.
Example:
1. Place your focus on the question phrase(s): **Q, Q, A.**
2. Place your focus on the answer(s): **Q, A, A.**

This is just a start. There any more ideas to come in the remainder of this course. Take some time and see how many 3 & 4 note Q & A phrases you can write. Also, after you have learned a technique or application in the upcoming sections, create new Q & A phrases by incorporating the new material you have learned.

SCALE NOTES AS CHORDS

Each scale note can be used as a chord. These chords will compliment each other just as the individual scale notes compliment each other. You can use these chords to write a rhythm progression, then use its individual scale notes to write leads and melodies over the chords.

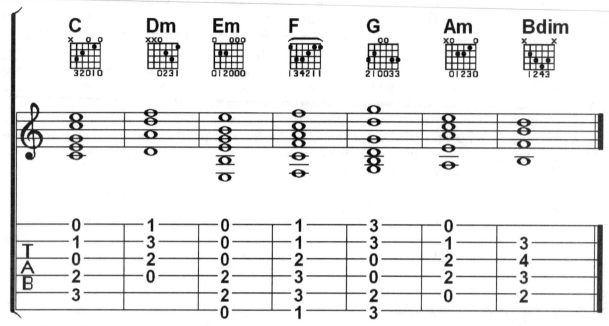

These are the major and minor chords taken from the key of C. The B diminished chord has an unusual tone so it is sometimes substituted with a B or Bm.

Swapping Majors and Minors

So far the chords we have used have all been built using only scale notes. In popular music, it is common to use the scale notes as chords, but change them from major chords to minors, or minor chords to majors. For example, blues and rock players often play A, D and E major chords, yet use the a minor scale for the lead guitar. The root or name of the chord is still derived from the scale, but the other notes in the chord may stray from the scale. Whenever you do this, or play a song that does this, the best rule is to let your ear guide you... If it sounds good to you, use it.

Power Chords (Rock & Metal Chords)

The same concept can be applied to power chords which are popular in rock and metal. These chords are built by using the combination of a scale note and its fifth tone up.

Just as scale notes can be used to compliment each other to write leads and solo's, chords can also be used together musically. Try different combinations for writing your own songs. By doing this you'll also hear familiar chord changes found in popular music. You can enhance your chord progressions by adding vocals or lead guitar using the same scale.

FORMULA FOR SONGWRITING

Once you have learned a scale, songwriting is very simple. First, your lead instrument, be it voice or guitar will use scale notes to create the main melody line. Then you can add harmony by following the melody line with other notes from the same scale. You can add a chord progression using chords derived from each scale note. You can add guitar fills throughout the song using scale notes, ...and even a guitar solo in the middle. All of this is done by using the same scale, which is also known as playing in key.

To learn more about chords and songwriting, check out Mark's book and CD set **GUITAR: Probable Chords** and new video **Easy Guitar Chords DVD**.

CHAPTER 5
APPLICATIONS

In this chapter we will cover scale applications to be used with each scale position you have learned. These applications are designed to enhance your playing and writing ability. Listen for these applications when you are listening to your favorite songs. You will find they are not just applied to the guitar. You will hear them in piano, voice, bass, as well as any other musical instruments.

1. INCREMENTS OF II

Breaking the scale into patterns of two. Begin with the 1st scale note then play the second. Next begin again on the 2nd note and end on the 3rd scale note. Play the 3rd scale note again, then end on the 4th. ETC...

So your pattern is $\boxed{1,2/2,3/3,4/4,5 \text{ etc...}}$

Allow each note to ring out for a full count. This application is written in 2/4 timing. There are 2 beats per measure. A quarter note receives 1 beat. Start out slowly. The count is 1-2 /1-2 /1-2 /1-2.

APPLY THIS APPLICATION TO EVERY SCALE POSITION

2. INCREMENTS OF III

Breaking the scale into patterns of three. Begin with the 1st, then 2nd scale note, and end on the 3rd. Begin again on the 2nd scale note, then the 3rd, end on the 4th. Start on the 3rd, then 4th, end on the 5th. 4th, 5th, end on the 6th. ETC...

So your pattern is 1,2,3/2,3,4/3,4,5/4,5,6/etc...

Allow each note to ring out for a full count. This application is written in 3/4 timing. There are 3 beats per measure. A quarter note receives one beat. Start slowly. The count is 1-2-3/1-2-3/1-2-3.

Pay close attention to major and minor root notes.

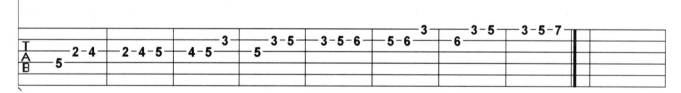

APPLY THIS APPLICATION TO EVERY SCALE POSITION

3. TWO STRINGS

Playing three scale notes on each string of any scale position. Break the scale into patterns of two strings. Starting with the 6th string, play notes 1, 2, & 3, followed by notes 4, 5, & 6 on the 5th string. Then repeat notes 4, 5, & 6 on the 5th string, adding notes 7, 8, & 9 on the 4th string. ETC...

So your pattern is 1,2,3,4,5,6/4,5,6,7,8,9/7,8,9,10,11,12/etc...

This application is written in 3/4 timing using eighth notes. There are 3 beats per measure. An eighth note receives half a beat. The count is 1-&-2-&-3-&/1-&-2-&-3-&/1-&-2-&-3-&.

COUNT: 1 & 2 & 3 &   1 & 2 & 3 &   1 & 2 & 3 &   1 & 2 & 3 &

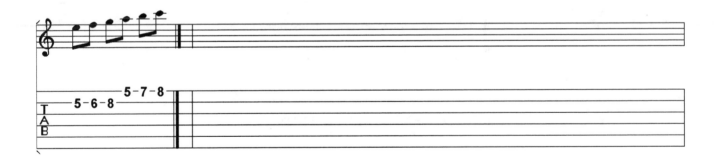

APPLY THIS APPLICATION TO EVERY SCALE POSITION

4. TWO STRINGS AND BACK (one note)

6th string notes 1, 2, & 3 followed by 5th string notes 4, 5, & 6 then back to note 5. Then repeat notes 4, 5, & 6 on the 5th string, adding notes 7, 8, 9, & back to 8 on the 4th string. ETC...

Pattern 1,2,3,4,5,6,5/4,5,6,7,8,9,8/7,8,9,10,11,12,11/etc...

This application is written in 4/4 timing using eighth notes and quarter notes. There are 4 beats per measure. An eighth note receives half a beat. A quarter note receives one beat. The count is 1-&-2-&-3-&-4/1-&-2-&-3-&-4/1-&-2-&-3-&-4.

COUNT: 1 & 2 & 3 & 4   1 & 2 & 3 & 4   1 & 2 & 3 & 4   1 & 2 & 3 & 4

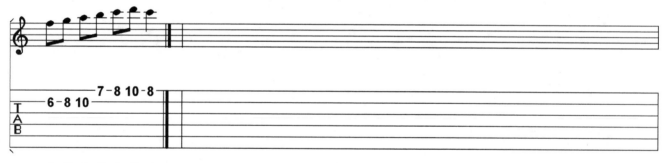

1 & 2 & 3 & 4

APPLY THIS APPLICATION TO EVERY SCALE POSITION

5. THREE STRINGS

Playing 3 scale notes on each string of any scale position. Break the scale into patterns of 3 strings (9 scale notes). Starting with the 6th string, play notes 1, 2, 3, followed by notes 4, 5, 6 on the 5th string, and 7, 8, 9 on the 4th string. Repeat notes 4, 5, 6 on the 5th string, 7, 8, 9 on the 4th string, adding notes 10, 11, & 12 on the 3rd string. ETC...

Pattern | 1,2,3,4,5,6,7,8,9/4,5,6,7,8,9,10,11,12/7,8,9,10,11,12,13,14,15/etc...

This application is written in 3/4 timing using triplets. Triplets are eighth notes written in groups of 3. A triplet receives a third of a beat. The count is 1-&-a- 2-&-a-3-&-a/1-&-a-2-&-a-3-&-a.

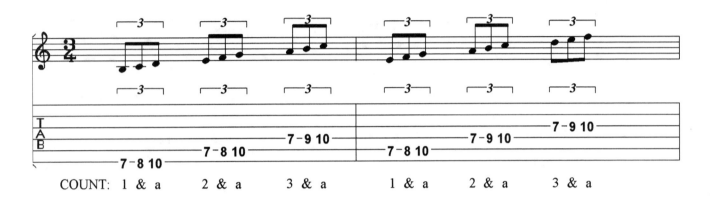

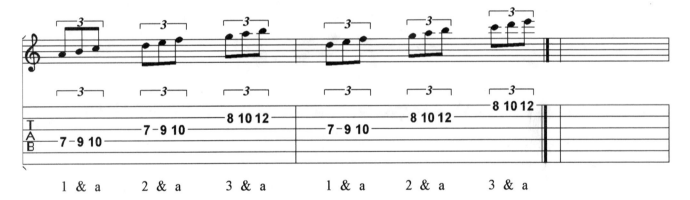

APPLY THREE STRINGS TO EVERY SCALE POSITION.

6. THREE STRINGS AND BACK (4 notes)

6th string, notes 1, 2, 3, 5th string notes 4, 5, 6, 4th string notes 7, 8, 9, back to 8, 7, then back to 6, & 5 on the 5th string. 5th string notes 4, 5, 6, 4th string notes 7, 8, 9, 3rd string notes 10, 11, 12, back to notes 11, 10, then 9, & 8 on the 4th string. ETC...

Pattern 1,2,3,4,5,6,7,8,9,8,7,6,5/4,5,6,7,8,9,10,11,12,11,10,9,8/7,8,9,10,11,12,13,14,15,14,13,12,11/etc...

This application is written in 4/4 timing using sixteenth notes, triplets, and eighth notes. A 16th note receives one quarter of a beat, a triplet receives one third of a beat, an eighth note receives half a beat. The count is 1-e-&-a-2-&-a-3-e-&-a-4-&/1-e-&-a-2-&-a-3-e-&-a-4-&.

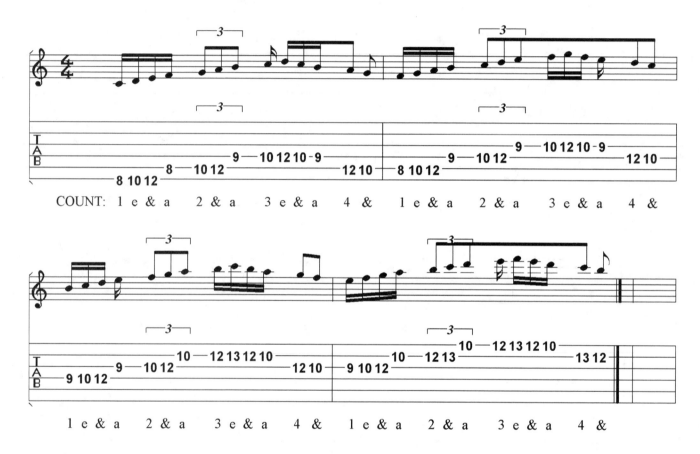

APPLY THIS APPLICATION TO EVERY SCALE POSITION, AND COMBINE IT WITH OTHER APPLICATIONS

7. INCREMENTS OF 4.

Breaking the scale into patterns of 4. Begin with the 6th string, notes 1, 2, 3 & on the 5th string note 4. Notes 2, & 3 on the 6th string, then notes 4, & 5 on the 5th string. The 3rd scale note on the 6th string, then notes 4, 5, & 6 on the 5th string. Notes 4, 5, 6, on the 5th string, then note 7 on the 4th string. ETC...

Pattern 1,2,3,4/2,3,4,5/3,4,5,6/4,5,6,7/5,6,7,8/etc...

This application is written in 4/4 timing using quarter notes. A quarter note receives one beat. The count is 1-2-3-4/1-2-3-4/1-2-3-4.

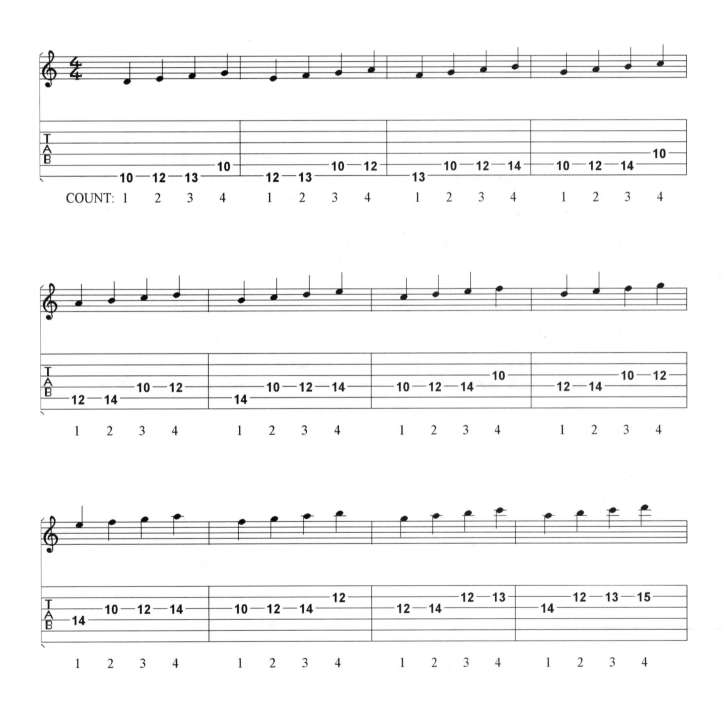

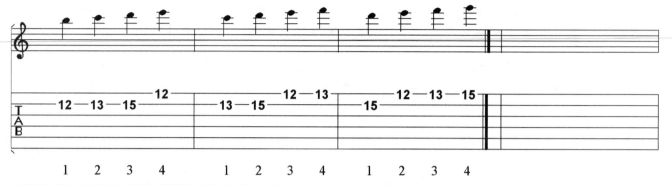

<table>
<thead></thead>
<tbody>
<tr><td>1</td><td>2</td><td>3</td><td>4</td><td>1</td><td>2</td><td>3</td><td>4</td><td>1</td><td>2</td><td>3</td><td>4</td></tr>
</tbody>
</table>

APPLY THIS APPLICATION TO EVERY SCALE POSITION, AND COMBINE IT WITH OTHER APPLICATIONS

To play the last application with eighth notes each note would receive half a beat. The count would be 1-&-2-&-3-&-4-&/1-&-2-&-3-&-4-&/1-&-2-&-3-&-4-&.

To play increments of 4 using sixteenth notes each note would receive a quarter of one beat. The count would be 1-e-&-a-2-e-&-a-3-e-&-a-4-e-&-a/1-e-&-a-2-e-&-a-3-e-&-a-4-e-&-a.

To play inc. of 4 in 3/4 timing you could play any combination of 2 quarter notes and 2 eighth notes. Using 2 quarter notes followed by 2 eighth notes, the count would be 1-2-3-&/1-2-3-&/1-2-3-&. Using a quarter note followed by 2 eighth notes, followed by a quarter note, the count would be 1-2-&-3/1-2-&-3/1-2-&-3.

YOU CAN APPLY ANY TIMING TO ANY NOTE OR GROUPS OF NOTES.
EXPERIMENT WITH DIFFERENT TIMINGS ON ALL APPLICATIONS.

8. INCREMENTS OF 4 AND BACK (1 note)

6th string notes 1, 2, 3, 5th string note 4, back to note 3 on the 6th string. 6th string notes 2, & 3, 5th string notes 4, & 5, back to note 4. 6th string note 3, 5th string notes 4, 5, 6, and back to note 5. 4, 5, & 6 on the 5th string, note 7 on the 4th string, then back to note 6 on the 5th string. ETC...

Pattern | 1,2,3,4,3/2,3,4,5,4/3,4,5,6,5/4,5,6,7,6/etc...

This pattern is written in 4/4 timing using quarter notes and eighth notes. A quarter note receives one beat, an eighth note receives half a beat. The count is 1-2-3-4-&/1-2-3-4-&/1-2-3-4-&.

COUNT: 1 2 3 4 &   1 2 3 4 &   1 2 3 4 &

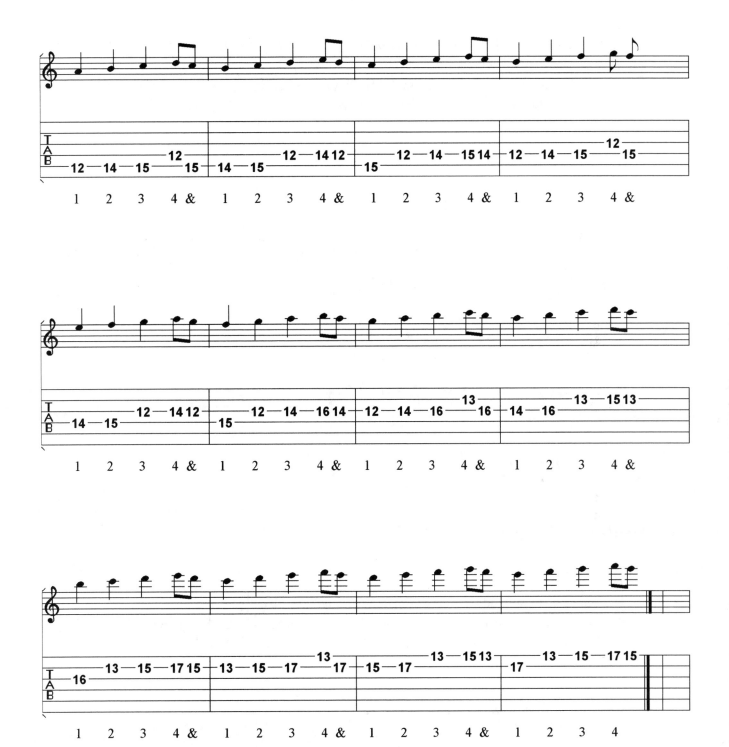

APPLY THIS APPLICATION TO EVERY SCALE POSITION, AND COMBINE IT WITH OTHER APPLICATIONS

9. STEP DOWN STEP UP

STEP DOWN

Starting with the 2nd note in any scale position followed by the 1st, then the 3rd followed by the 2nd, 4th then 3rd, 5th then 4th. ETC...   Pattern 2,1/3,2/4,3/5,4/6,5/7,6/etc...

This application is written in 2/4 timing using quarter notes. There are 2 beats per measure, a quarter note receives one beat. The count is 1,2/1,2/1,2/1,2.

STEP UP

The opposite of step down.   Pattern 7,8/6,7/5,6/4,5/3,4/etc...

This application is written in 4/4 timing using eighth notes. An eighth note receives half a beat. The count is 1-&-2-&-3-&-4-&/1-&-2-&-3-&-4-&/1-&-2-&-3-&-4-&.

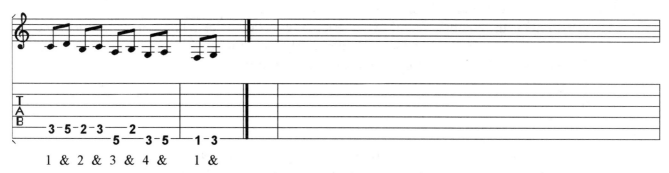

1 & 2 & 3 & 4 & 1 &

APPLY STEP DOWN/STEP UP TO EVERY SCALE POSITION, AND COMBINE IT WITH OTHER APPLICATIONS

RHYTHM EXPERIMENTATION

Earlier in this chapter I suggested that you try playing these applications with different rhythms. Here are some basic principles to help you further explore timing. This chart will show you the breakdown of notes from whole to sixteenth notes in 4/4 timing, (4 beats per measure).

Whole	Half	Quarter	Eighth	Sixteenth
4 beats	2 beats	1 beat	1/2 beat	1/4 beat

This example is written in 4/4 timing. A rhythm can use any combination of the above note types as long as the total count equals 4 complete beats. The following are some examples of rhythm combinations, using half and quarter notes. Notice that each measure equals 4 beats.

HALF AND QUARTER NOTES

Rhythm 1.	Rhythm 2.	Rhythm 3.
half quarter quarter	quarter half quarter	quarter quarter half

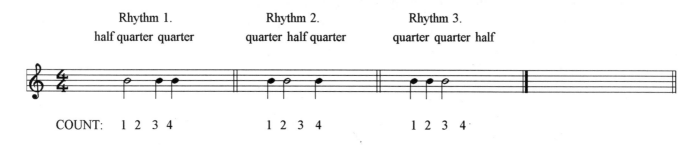

COUNT: 1 2 3 4   1 2 3 4   1 2 3 4

In rhythm 1, the combination is half, quarter, quarter, so the first note is held the longest. Technical Breakdown: Hold the half note for counts 1 and 2, play a quarter note for the 3 count, play a quarter note for the 4 count. Total beats = 4. You can repeat this rhythm over and over again. It can be applied to a single note, scale notes, scale applications, chords, etc...

Rhythm 2 is the combination of quarter, half, quarter. The second note is held the longest. Technical Breakdown: Hold the quarter note for count 1, half note for counts 2 and 3, hold a quarter note for the 4 count. Total beats = 4.

Rhythm 3 is the combination of two quarter notes followed by a half note. The third note is held the longest. Technical Breakdown: Hold a quarter note for beat 1, hold a quarter note for beat 2, and hold the half note for beats 3 and 4. Total beats = 4.

EIGHTH NOTES

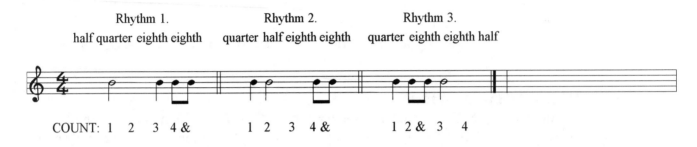

| Rhythm 1. | Rhythm 2. | Rhythm 3. |
| half quarter eighth eighth | quarter half eighth eighth | quarter eighth eighth half |

COUNT: 1   2   3   4 &   1   2   3   4 &   1 2 & 3   4

Eighth notes equal half a beat, so each count needs to be separated into two pulses. Instead of using a basic count: 1 2 3 4, eighth notes are counted: 1 & 2 & 3 & 4 &.

Quarter Notes: 1   2   3   4

Eighth Notes: 1   &   2   &   3   &   4   &

In rhythm 1, the combination is half, quarter, eighth, eighth. Because the 4th beat consists of 2 eighth notes it needs to be split into two accents. Instead of counting the fourth beat as 4, you need to count it as "4 &." Technical Breakdown: Hold the half note for counts 1 and 2, play a quarter note for the 3 count, play an eighth note for the 4 count, play an eighth note for the "&" count. Total beats = 4.

Rhythm 2 is the combination of quarter, half, eighth, eighth. Again the 4 count is split into 2 accents to accommodate the 2 eighth notes. Technical Breakdown: Hold the quarter note for count 1, hold the half note for counts 2 and 3, hold an eighth note for 4, hold an eighth note for "&."

Rhythm 3 is the combination of quarter, eighth, eighth, half. There are two eighth notes in the space of the two count so it is split into 2 accents, (2 &). Technical Breakdown: Hold the quarter note for the 1 count, hold an eighth note for 2, hold an eighth note for "&," hold the half note for beats 3 and 4.

SIXTEENTH NOTES

This rhythm example uses half, quarter, eighth, and sixteenth notes.

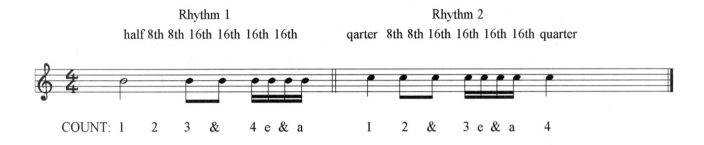

Sixteenth notes equal a quarter of a beat, so each count needs to be separated into 4 pulses.
Quarter Notes: 1   2   3   4
Eighth Notes: 1   &   2   &   3   &   4   &
Sixteenth Notes: 1 e & a 2 e & a 3 e & a 4 e & a

In rhythm 1, the combination is half, eighth, eighth, sixteenth, sixteenth, sixteenth, sixteenth. Because the 4th beat consists of four sixteenth notes it needs to be split into four accents. Instead of counting the fourth beat as 4, you need to count it as "4 e & a." Technical Breakdown: Hold the half note for counts 1 and 2, play an eighth note for the 3 count, play an eighth note for the & count, play a sixteenth note for the 4 count, play a sixteenth note for the "e" count, play a sixteenth note for the "&" count, and play a sixteenth note for the "a" count. Total beats = 4.

Rhythm 2 is a combination of quarter, eighth, eighth, sixteenth, sixteenth, sixteenth, sixteenth, quarter. There are 4 sixteenth notes in the space of the 3 count so it is split up into four accents, (3 e & a). Technical Breakdown: Hold the quarter note for the 1 count, hold an eighth note for the 2 count, hold an eighth note for the "&" count, hold a sixteenth note for the 3 count, play a sixteenth note for the "e" count, play a sixteenth note for the "&" count, play a sixteenth note for the "a" count, play a quarter note for the 4 count. Total beats = 4.

CHAPTER 6
TECHNIQUES

    To be able to play notes is one thing. But, to move a listener, or even yourself as a player, you need to do more than just play a note. You need to give it life. Although there is no substitute for "soul", learning and using techniques will certainly help you achieve the status quicker. The techniques offered in this book are intended to give life to your music. As I progressed as a musician I began to realize that a single note is just as important, if not more important than any group of notes. Give your music life. Give each note you play an emotion. When you play the notes in this book, listen for an emotion or feeling. They are not pre-determined. There is no wrong or right emotion. It is open to what you hear and feel. This is what music is. And this is your journey to become a better musician.

1. **DOUBLE PICKING**
    Pick each note twice.

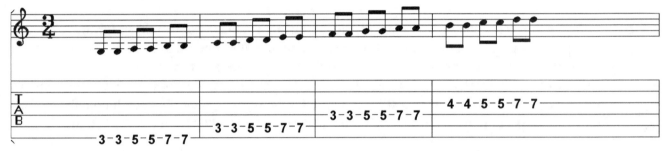

COUNT: 1 & 2 & 3 & etc...

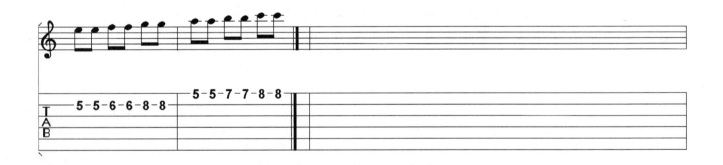

NOW APPLY THIS TECHNIQUE TO EVERY SCALE POSITION, APPLICATION, AND RHYTHM.

2. PALM MUTE

   Achieved by resting the palm of your picking hand on the string(s) you are picking. You can also use your pinkie as an extension of your palm to mute the higher strings if your palm doesn't cover all six. You can alter the duration of each note by moving your palm closer to or farther from the bridge while playing. The symbol for using the palm mute technique is P.M., followed by a dotted line. The dotted line will extend for as long as you are required to apply the palm mute.   P.M.................................

Notice the break in the third measure where the B note, (5th string 2nd fret), is not palm muted.

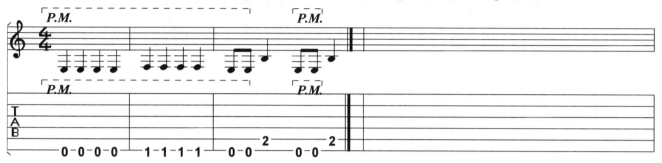

NOW APPLY THIS TECHNIQUE TO EVERY SCALE POSITION, APPLICATION, RHYTHM, AND COMBINATION OF THE FOUR.

TECH/APP COMBINATION
APPLICATION INC. OF III THEN IV
TECHNIQUE DOUBLE PICKING & PALM MUTE

   This combination is written in 4/4 timing using triplets and sixteenth notes. The count is 1-&-a-2-&-a-3-e-&-a-4-e-&-a/1-&-a-2-&-a-3-e-&-a-4-e-&-a/1-&-a-2-&-a-3-e-&-a-4-e-&-a.

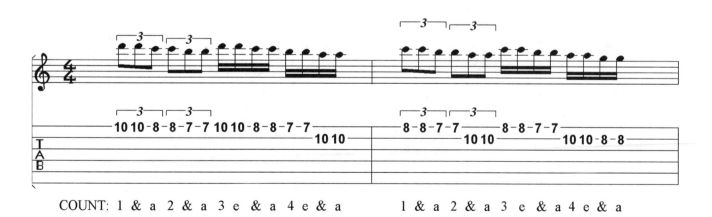

COUNT: 1 & a 2 & a 3 e & a 4 e & a   1 & a 2 & a 3 e & a 4 e & a

1 & a 2 & a 3 e & a 4 e & a   1 & a 2 & a 3 e & a 4 e & a

1 & a 2 & a 3 e & a 4 e & a   1 & a 2 & a 3 e & a 4 e & a

1 & a 2 & a 3 e & a 4 e & a   1 & a 2 & a 3 e & a 4 e & a

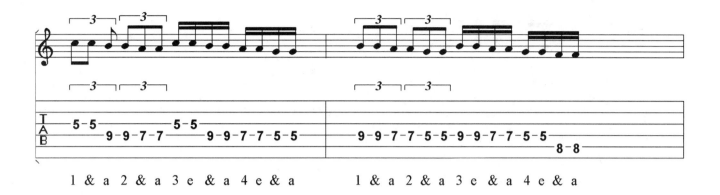

1 & a 2 & a 3 e & a 4 e & a   1 & a 2 & a 3 e & a 4 e & a

1 & a 2 & a 3 e & a 4 e & a   1 & a 2 & a 3 e & a 4 e & a

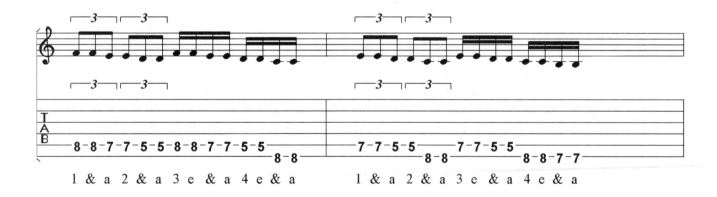

1 & a 2 & a 3 e & a 4 e & a   1 & a 2 & a 3 e & a 4 e & a

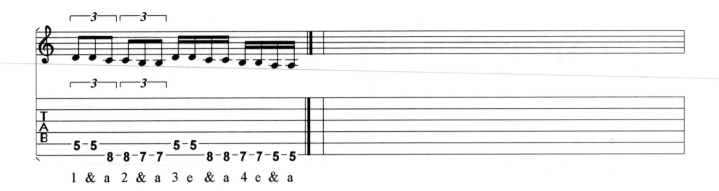

1 & a 2 & a 3 e & a 4 e & a

NOW APPLY THIS TECHNIQUE TO EVERY SCALE POSITION, APPLICATION, RHYTHM, AND COMBINATION OF THE FOUR.

3. VIBRATO

This technique is excellent for building strength. It is achieved by continuously bending the note and returning it to its original pitch. Apply this technique, allow the thumb of your playing hand to hang over the neck of your guitar, above your middle finger. Use the appropriate playing finger to hold the note you are playing. Bend or "shake" the string by twisting your forearm. Do not bend your wrist, and do not bend the string by bending your fingers! You may find it difficult to apply vibrato with your pinkie, if so, substitute those notes with your ring finger by sliding it up to whichever note you want to play.

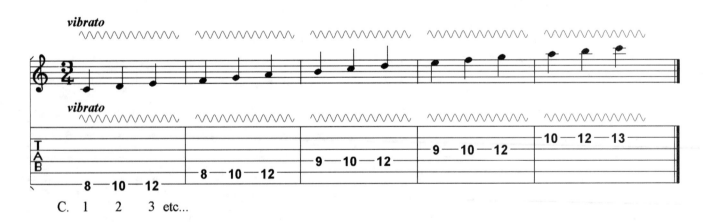

C. 1 2 3 etc...

Vibrato is difficult to achieve on the 1st string of most guitars.

NOW APPLY THIS TECHNIQUE TO EVERY SCALE POSITION, APPLICATION, RHYTHM, AND COMBINATION OF THE FOUR.

4. PASSING TONES

Non scale notes played between scale notes. Passing tones can be used to connect two scale notes. Passing tones may not sound desirable out of sequence. In this exercise the initials "p.t." have been placed above each passing tone.

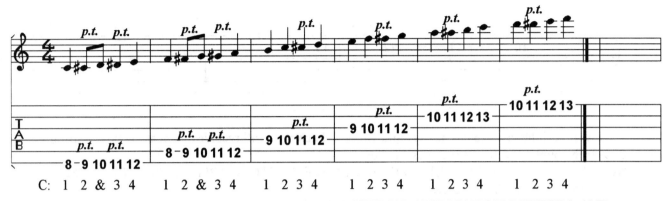

NOW APPLY THIS TECHNIQUE TO EVERY SCALE POSITION, APPLICATION, RHYTHM, AND COMBINATION OF THE FOUR.

TECH/APP COMBO
PASSING TONES WITH VIBRATO

Play this exercise at a slow pace, holding each note for a 4 count, bending the string for each count.

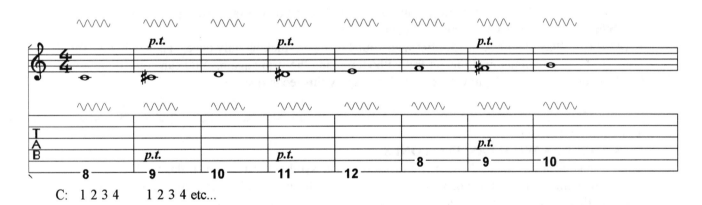

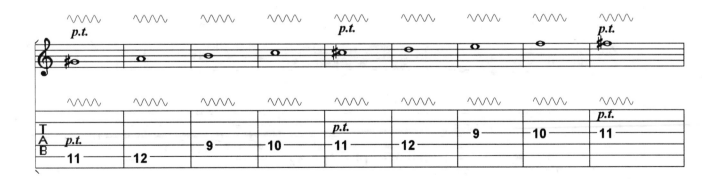

[Musical notation with staff showing whole notes with vibrato marks (∿∿∿) and "p.t." markings, accompanied by TAB staff reading:]

```
∿∿    ∿∿    ∿∿    ∿∿    ∿∿    ∿∿    ∿∿    ∿∿    ∿∿
                                    10    11    12    13
      10    11    12    13
  12                            p.t.
            p.t.
```

Now repeat the last exercise using rapid vibrato. Each note will receive one beat, bend the string for each 16th count so each note receives 4 bends.
NOW APPLY THIS TECHNIQUE TO EVERY SCALE POSITION, APPLICATION, RHYTHM, AND COMBINATION OF THE FOUR.

5. HAMMER ON

Achieved by picking a note then "hammering" a higher fret on the same string with your free finger(s) to produce another note without picking again.
EXAMPLE: Play the 6th string 5th fret with your 1st finger, picking only once. Then using the tip of your 3rd finger, hammer onto the 7th fret without picking the string again. You can control the sound level of your hammer on by how hard or soft you apply this technique.

TECH/APP COMBO
HAMMER ONS WITH PASSING TONES
There is a slide at the end of the first two measures. The symbol for a slide is a slash, with "sl" above it.
Slides are achieved by sliding your finger up or down the fretboard, while holding a note. In the piece below slide the 11th fret notes to the 12th fret on the sixth and fifth string.

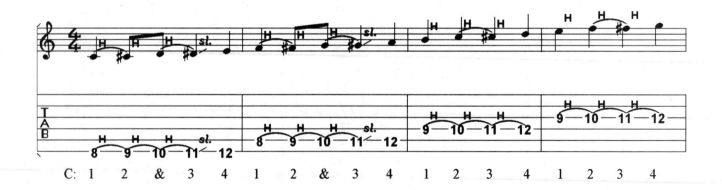

```
C:  1    2    &    3    4    1    2    &    3    4    1    2    3    4    1    2    3    4
```

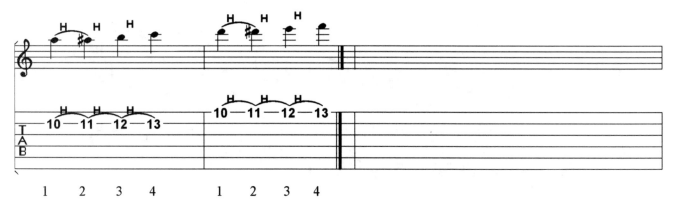

1   2   3   4   1   2   3   4

NOW APPLY THIS TECHNIQUE TO EVERY SCALE POSITION, APPLICATION, RHYTHM, AND COMBINATION OF THE FOUR.

TECH/APP COMBO
HAMMER ONS WITH INC OF II

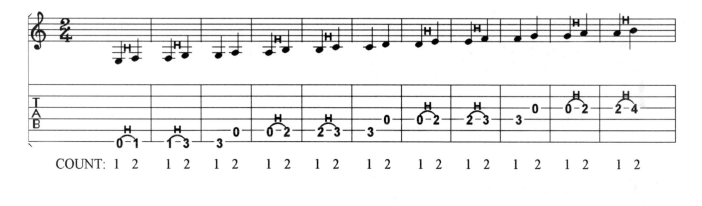

COUNT: 1   2   1   2   1   2   1   2   1   2   1   2   1   2   1   2   1   2   1   2   1   2   1   2

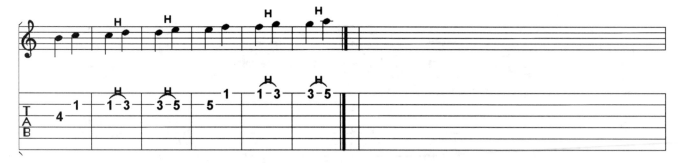

NOW APPLY THIS TECHNIQUE TO EVERY SCALE POSITION, APPLICATION, RHYTHM, AND COMBINATION OF THE FOUR.
TECH/APP COMBO

HAMMER ONS WITH TWO STRINGS

COUNT: 1 & 2 & 3 &   1 & 2 & 3 &   1 & 2 & 3 &   1 & 2 & 3 &

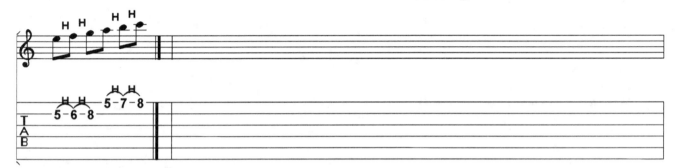

1 & 2 & 3 &

NOW APPLY THIS TECHNIQUE TO EVERY SCALE POSITION, APPLICATION, RHYTHM, AND
COMBINATION OF THE FOUR.

TECH/APP COMBO
HAMMER ONS AND THREE STRINGS

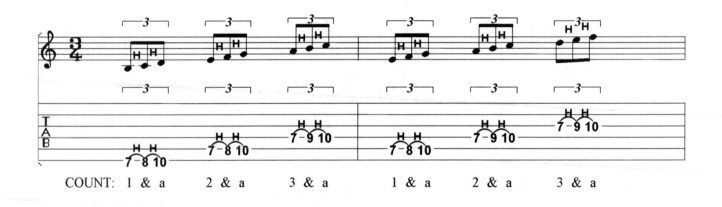

COUNT: 1 & a   2 & a   3 & a   1 & a   2 & a   3 & a

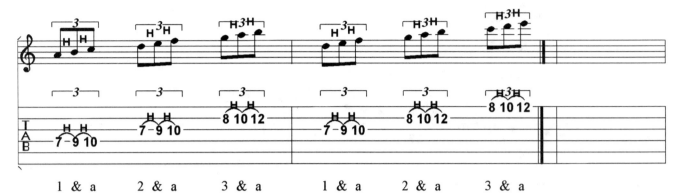

1 & a   2 & a   3 & a   1 & a   2 & a   3 & a

NOW APPLY THIS TECHNIQUE TO EVERY SCALE POSITION, APPLICATION, RHYTHM, AND COMBINATION OF THE FOUR.

TECH/APP COMBO
HAMMER ONS AND INC OF III

COUNT: 1 2 3   1 2 3   1 2 3   1 2 3   1 2 3   1 2 3   1 2 3   1 2 3

1 2 3   1 2 3   1 2 3   1 2 3   1 2 3   1 2 3   1 2 3   1 2 3

NOW APPLY THIS TECHNIQUE TO EVERY SCALE POSITION, APPLICATION, RHYTHM, AND COMBINATION OF THE FOUR.

CHAPTER 7
ABOVE THE 12 FRET
THE OCTAVE POSITIONS

F OR 4TH POSITION

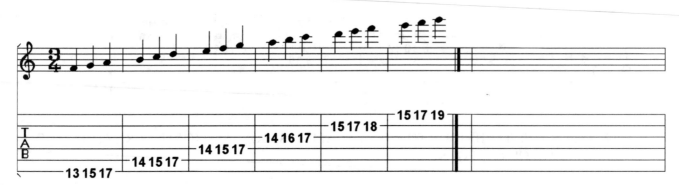

APPLY EVERY TECHNIQUE, APPLICATION, RHYTHM, AND COMBINATION OF THE THREE TO THIS
SCALE POSITION.

G OR 5TH POSITION

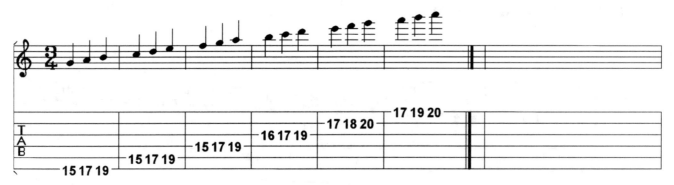

APPLY EVERY TECHNIQUE, APPLICATION, RHYTHM, AND COMBINATION OF THE THREE TO THIS
SCALE POSITION.

A OR 6TH POSITION. 1ST POSITION MINOR ROOT

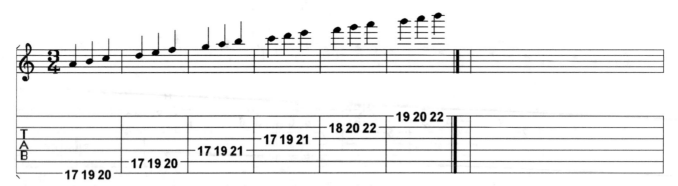

APPLY EVERY TECHNIQUE, APPLICATION, RHYTHM, AND COMBINATION OF THE THREE TO THIS
SCALE POSITION.
B OR 7TH POSITION

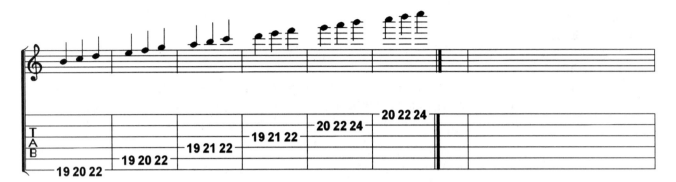

APPLY EVERY TECHNIQUE, APPLICATION, RHYTHM, AND COMBINATION OF THE THREE TO THIS SCALE POSITION.

C OR 1ST POSITION MAJOR ROOT

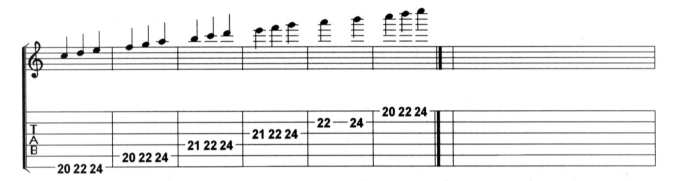

APPLY EVERY TECHNIQUE, APPLICATION, RHYTHM, AND COMBINATION OF THE THREE TO THIS SCALE POSITION.

CHAPTER 8
MORE TECHNIQUES

6. PULL OFFS

The opposite of a hammer on. Pull offs are achieved by picking a fretted note then pulling the finger you are using to fret that note away from the fretboard at a 45 degree angle, producing a lower pitched note on the same string without picking it. The note being produced by the pull off can be fretted or open.

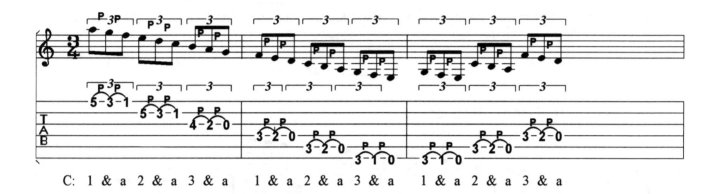

C: 1 & a 2 & a 3 & a   1 & a 2 & a 3 & a   1 & a 2 & a 3 & a

1 & a 2 & a 3 & a

APPLY THIS TECHNIQUE TO EVERY SCALE POSITION, APPLICATION, RHYTHM, AND COMBINATION OF THE FOUR.

THE HAMMER ON PULL OFF COMBINATIONS
7. HAMMER PULL/PULL HAMMER

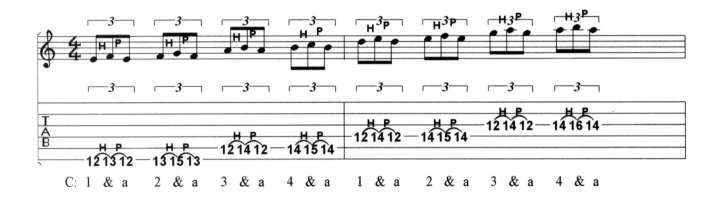

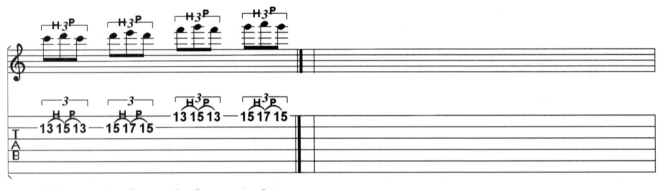

APPLY THIS TECHNIQUE TO EVERY SCALE POSITION, APPLICATION, RHYTHM, AND COMBINATION OF THE FOUR.

TECH/APP COMBO
HAMMER PULL WITH INC OF III

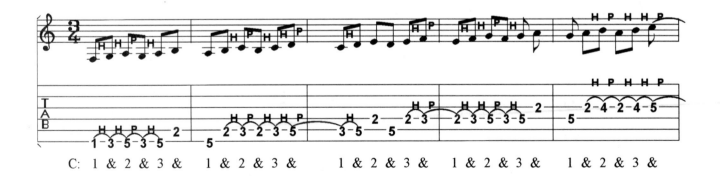

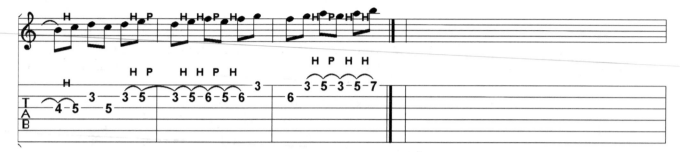

1 & 2 & 3 &   1 & 2 & 3 &   1 & 2 & 3 &

APPLY THIS TECHNIQUE TO EVERY SCALE POSITION, APPLICATION, RHYTHM, AND COMBINATION OF THE FOUR.

8. **SLIDE**

Achieved by picking a fretted note and sliding it, without releasing pressure, up or down the string to another note.

TECH/APP COMBO
SLIDE WITH INC OF III

C: 1   2   3   4   1   2   3   4   1   2   3   4   1   2   3   4

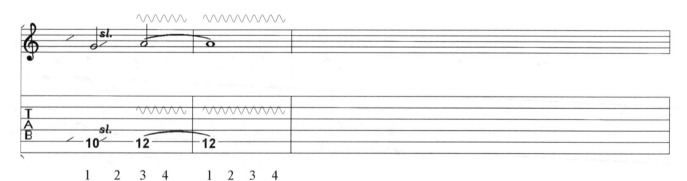

1   2   3   4   1   2   3   4

APPLY THIS TECHNIQUE TO EVERY SCALE POSITION, APPLICATION, RHYTHM, AND COMBINATION OF THE FOUR.

FOUR NOTES PER STRING WITH SLIDE

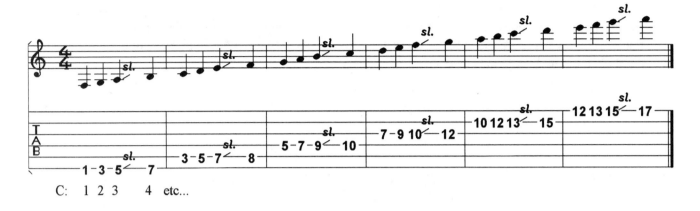

C: 1 2 3   4 etc...

APPLY THIS TECHNIQUE TO EVERY SCALE POSITION, APPLICATION, RHYTHM, AND COMBINATION OF THE FOUR.

9. VOLUME SWELLS

This technique is limited to the electric guitar. It gives the guitar a violin sound. It is achieved by playing a note with your guitars volume knob off, then increase the volume while holding the note.

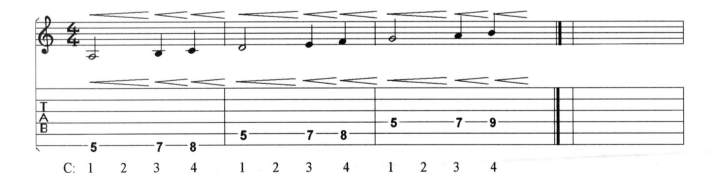

C: 1   2   3   4   1   2   3   4   1   2   3   4

APPLY THIS TECHNIQUE TO EVERY SCALE POSITION, APPLICATION, RHYTHM, AND COMBINATION OF THE FOUR.

RHYTHM EXPERIMENTATION II: NOTES AND RESTS

Music is made up of more than notes. Sometimes the lack of notes can make a piece stand out. Just as there are symbols for the notes you play, there are also symbols for the times when you don't play notes. These symbols are called rests. There are rest symbols for every note symbol. Here is a comparison chart for notes and their equal rests.

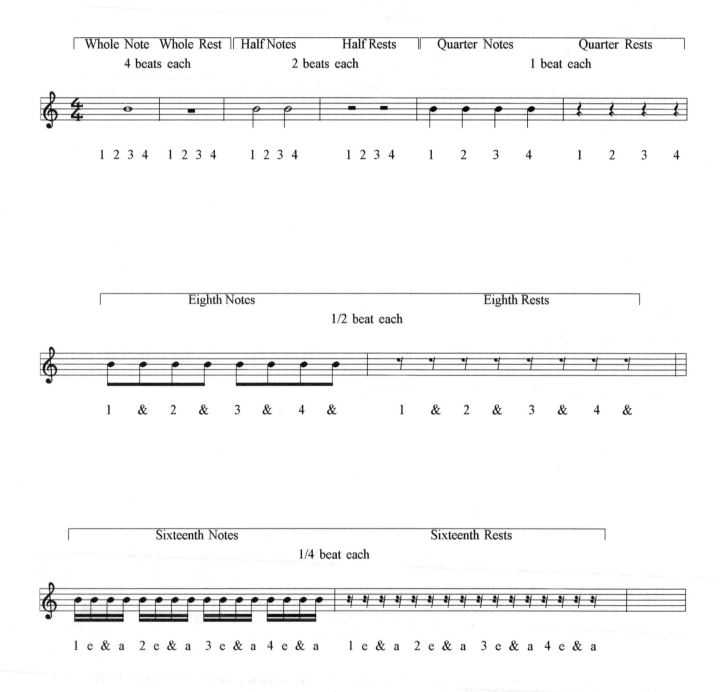

Here are some basic rhythms combining notes and rests. Repeat each rhythm over and over again until you are comfortable playing it. At first apply each rhythm to one note. When you can play a rhythm smoothly, then apply it to chords and multiple scale notes.

10. DAMPING

Used to end the duration of the note being played. EXAMPLE: Pick the 6th string 1st fret. When the note has sounded release the pressure of your finger just enough so the note is stopped. Make sure your finger is still touching the string when you so this. If you lift your finger completely away from the string you may cause an unwanted note to sound.

Another way to dampen a string is to rest the palm of your picking hand on the string after the note has been sounded.

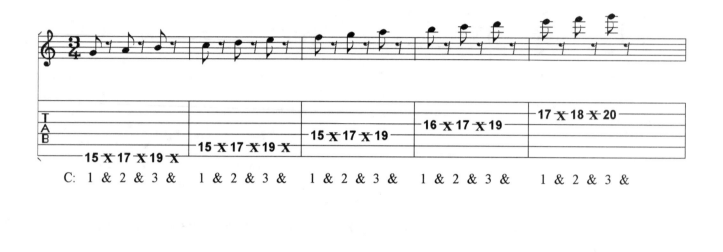

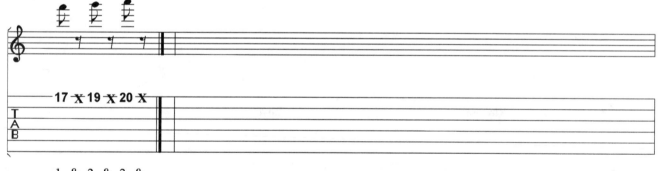

APPLY THIS TECHNIQUE TO EVERY SCALE POSITION, APPLICATION, RHYTHM, AND COMBINATION OF THE FOUR.

11. HARMONICS

Harmonics produce a chime like sound. It is achieved by placing your finger just above the indicated fret on the string you are picking. Do not apply pressure to the string, and do not allow any other fingers to touch the string. In fact, after the harmonic is picked, you can pull your hand(s) completely away from the string(s).

Natural harmonics can only be achieved on the nut(open notes), 5th fret, 7th, 12th, 17th, 19th, & 24th frets.

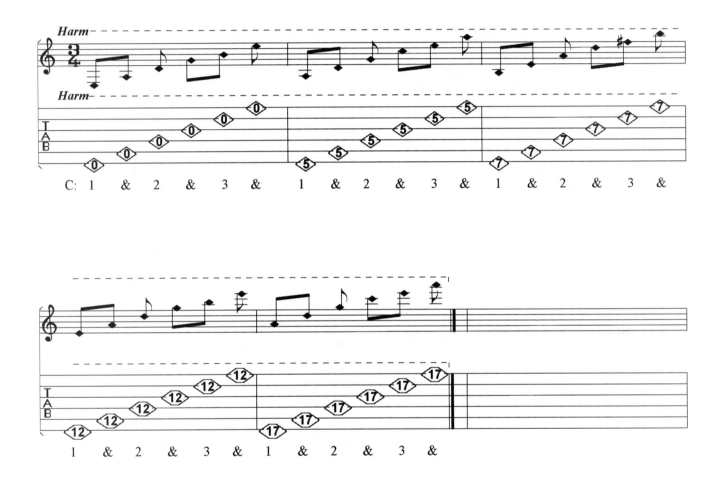

NOW APPLY THIS TECHNIQUE TO EVERY SCALE POSITION, APPLICATION, RHYTHM, AND COMBINATION OF THE FOUR.

Take some time to experiment with harmonics above other frets. You will find that you can achieve natural harmonics in other areas on the string. However, they will not sound as clear as the notes that have been given.

12. ARTIFICIAL HARMONICS/ NOTE SQUEAL

Achieved by fretting a note, and with your picking hand, allow the edge of your thumb to touch the string when you pick it. This will produce a higher (squealing) pitch to the note you have played.

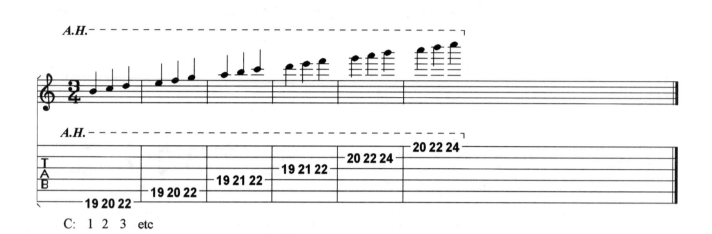

C: 1 2 3 etc

APPLY THIS TECHNIQUE TO EVERY SCALE POSITION, APPLICATION, RHYTHM, AND COMBINATION OF THE FOUR.

VIBRATO AND A.H. COMBO

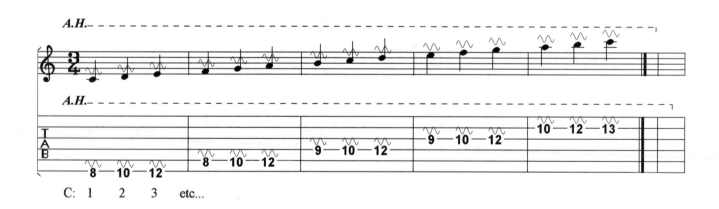

C: 1   2   3   etc...

APPLY THIS TECHNIQUE TO EVERY SCALE POSITION, APPLICATION, RHYTHM, AND COMBINATION OF THE FOUR.

13. PICKING HAND ARTIFICIAL HARMONICS/ PALM HARMONICS

Use a finger or the palm of your picking hand to lightly touch the string *12 frets above a fretted note while picking that note.

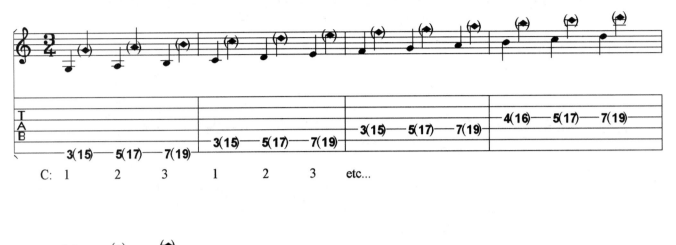

*You can also achieve palm harmonics on other areas of the string. Most noticeable harmonics are produced 5, 7, 12, 17, 19, & 24 frets above the fretted note.
APPLY THIS TECHNIQUE TO EVERY SCALE POSITION, APPLICATION, RHYTHM, AND COMBINATION OF THE FOUR.

14. TREMOLO PICKING

Achieved by picking a note rapidly.

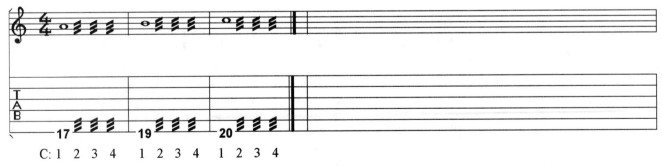

APPLY THIS TECHNIQUE TO EVERY SCALE POSITION, APPLICATION, RHYTHM, AND COMBINATION OF THE FOUR.

CHAPTER 9
TAPPING

Achieved by using the index or middle finger of your picking hand to hammer/tap onto a fret, producing a pitch, then pull off to an open or fretted note. The musical notation for tapping is a +, (plus sign), or a T.

TAP HAMMER

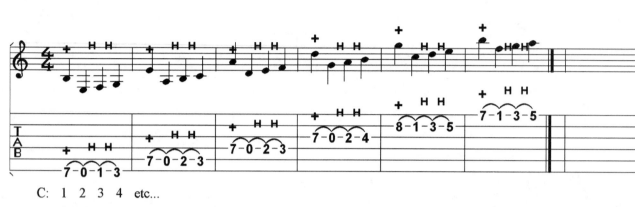

C: 1 2 3 4 etc...

APPLY THIS TECHNIQUE TO EVERY SCALE POSITION, APPLICATION, RHYTHM, AND COMBINATION OF THE FOUR.

In this example we will move our tapping finger while our fretboard fingers play the same notes.

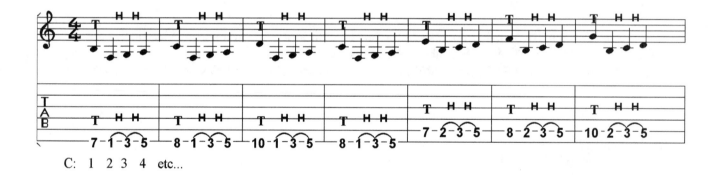

C: 1 2 3 4 etc...

APPLY THIS TECHNIQUE TO EVERY SCALE POSITION, APPLICATION, RHYTHM, AND COMBINATION OF THE FOUR.

Here we will move our fretboard fingers while our tapping finger plays the same note.

APPLY THIS TECHNIQUE TO EVERY SCALE POSITION, APPLICATION, RHYTHM, AND COMBINATION OF THE FOUR.

TAP PULL HAMMER

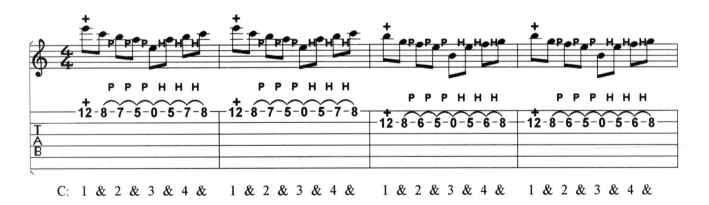

1 & 2 & 3 & 4 &   1 & 2 & 3 & 4 &

APPLY THIS TECHNIQUE TO EVERY SCALE POSITION, APPLICATION, RHYTHM, AND COMBINATION OF THE FOUR.

TAP HAMMER TAP PULL

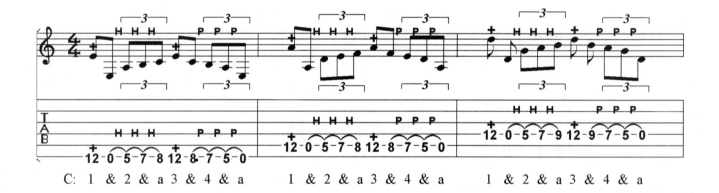

C: 1 & 2 & a 3 & 4 & a   1 & 2 & a 3 & 4 & a   1 & 2 & a 3 & 4 & a

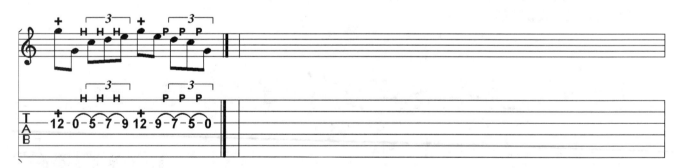

1 & 2 & a 3 & 4 & a

APPLY THIS TECHNIQUE TO EVERY SCALE POSITION, APPLICATION, RHYTHM, AND COMBINATION OF THE FOUR.

We are unlimited when it comes to mixing scales, applications, patterns, and rhythms. Take what you have learned and find a way to mix it with tapping.

TAPPING HARMONICS

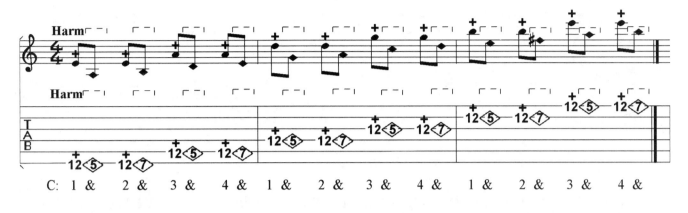

APPLY THIS TECHNIQUE TO EVERY SCALE POSITION, APPLICATION, RHYTHM, AND COMBINATION OF THE FOUR.

TAP HAMMER TECHNIQUES
TAP HAMMER TECHNIQUE APPLIED SO THE TAPPING HAND FOLLOWS THE FRET HAND AS IT MOVES DOWN IN PITCH IN MOVEMENTS OF II...

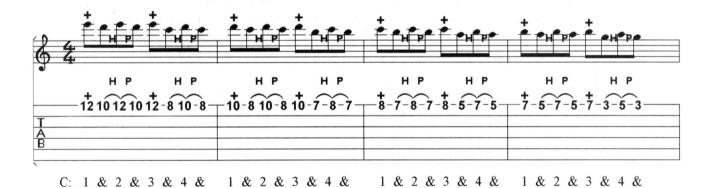

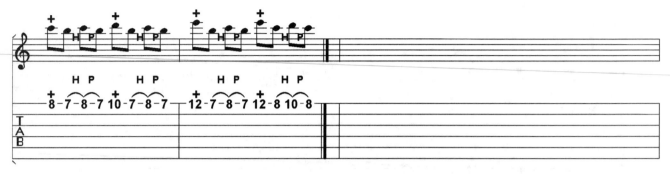

1 & 2 & 3 & 4 &   1 & 2 & 3 & 4 &

APPLY THIS TECHNIQUE TO EVERY SCALE POSITION, APPLICATION, RHYTHM, AND COMBINATION OF THE FOUR.

APPLY TAPPING TO DIFFERENT POSITIONS

1. You can leave your fretboard hand in the same spot, but move your tapping hand to a new position.

2. Use your tapping hand on the same fret, but move your fretboard hand.

3. Lengthen or shorten the distance between your tapping and fretboard hands.
    There are an infinite number of possibilities when it comes to tapping. Spend some serious time exploring the possibilities of tapping. Use your own creativity to combine scale notes, different strings, techniques, applications, rhythms, and even picking techniques along with your tapping.

CHAPTER 10

STRING BENDING

Use this technique to alter the pitch of a note by bending the string with your fingers. To apply this technique allow the thumb of your fretboard hand to hang over the neck of your guitar, above your middle finger. The note you wish to bend should (in most cases) be fretted by your ring/3rd finger with your middle finger on the fret behind it for assistance. As your fingers get stronger you may not find this necessary. Your index finger is used to lay across the other strings to prevent stray notes.
EXAMPLE: If you were to bend the 8th fret of the 2nd string, your 3rd finger would be placed on the 8th fret, your 2nd finger would be placed on the 7th fret, your index/1st finger would lay lightly across the 1st, 2nd, 3rd, & possibly the 4th string. Your thumb would hang over the neck of your guitar, above your 2nd finger on the 7th fret.

To stay in key when bending strings, you must bend in scale degrees. Scale degrees are half steps, whole steps, 1 ½ steps, 2 steps, etc...   A half step is equal to one fret.
EXAMPLE: If you are playing the natural scale and you want to bend a B note; You would bend the note a ½ step to sound a C note, 1 ½ steps for a D note, 2 ½ steps for an E note. If you bend a string to high your string will break. A 2 ½ is usually the highest you will ever bend a note.

Listen closely to your string bending and learn the difference between the different scale degrees.

SOME HELPFUL GUIDELINES FOR STRING BENDING
½ STEP BEND = 1 FRET
1 STEP BEND = 2 FRETS
1 ½ STEP BEND = 3 FRETS
2 STEP BEND = 4 FRETS
ETC...
ALSO, WHEN BENDING ON THE 1ST, 2ND, & 3RD STRINGS, BEND THE STRING UP.
BEND THE STRING DOWNWARD FOR STRINGS 6, 5, & 4.

1. **HALF STEP BENDS**
   This exercise is designed to get your ear used to hearing half step degrees.

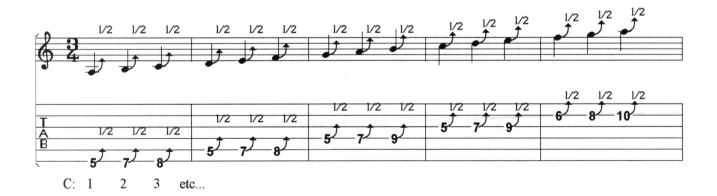

C: 1   2   3   etc...

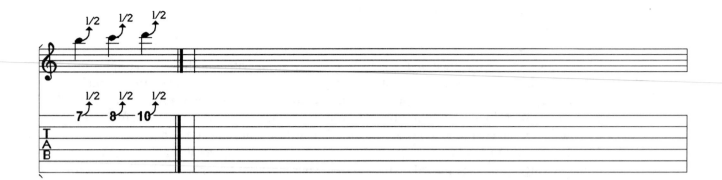

APPLY THIS TECHNIQUE TO EVERY SCALE POSITION, APPLICATION, RHYTHM, AND
COMBINATION OF THE FOUR.

2. **WHOLE STEP BENDS**

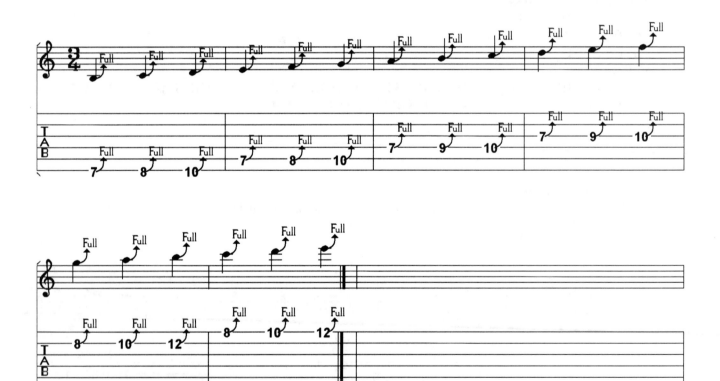

APPLY THIS TECHNIQUE TO EVERY SCALE POSITION, APPLICATION, RHYTHM, AND
COMBINATION OF THE FOUR.

3. ONE AND ONE HALF STEP BENDS

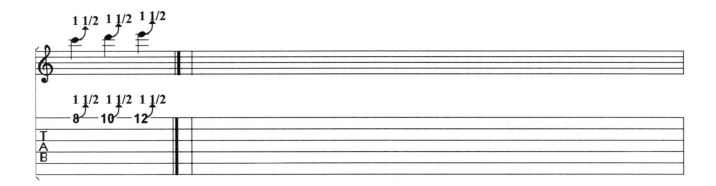

APPLY THIS TECHNIQUE TO EVERY SCALE POSITION, APPLICATION, RHYTHM, AND
COMBINATION OF THE FOUR.

4. BENDING TO THE NEXT SCALE NOTE
To stay within proper pitch you will have to mix ½ & 1 step bends.

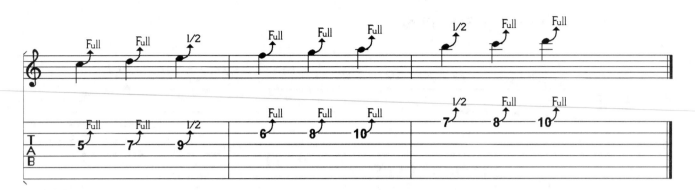

APPLY THIS TECHNIQUE TO EVERY SCALE POSITION, APPLICATION, RHYTHM, AND COMBINATION OF THE FOUR.

THE APPLICATIONS OF BENDING

Bending is a technique with many applications. You can create several interesting phrases by bending a single note.

1. BEND AND RELEASE

APPLY THIS TECHNIQUE TO EVERY SCALE POSITION, APPLICATION, RHYTHM, AND COMBINATION OF THE FOUR.

2. PRE-BEND

Bend the note before picking .

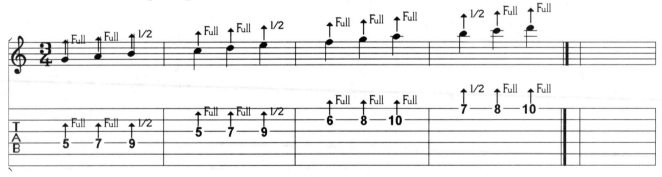

APPLY THIS TECHNIQUE TO EVERY SCALE POSITION, APPLICATION, RHYTHM, AND COMBINATION OF THE FOUR.

3. PRE-BEND AND RELEASE

Bend the note, pick the note, then steadily release the bend while the note rings out.

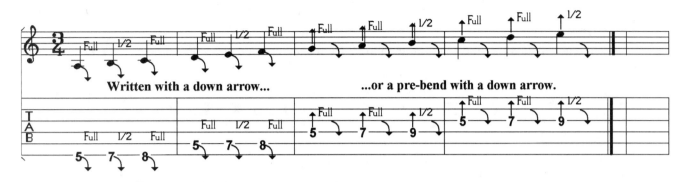

4. GHOST BEND (FOR ELECTRIC GUITAR)

Pick the note with the guitar volume off, increase the volume while you bend the note.

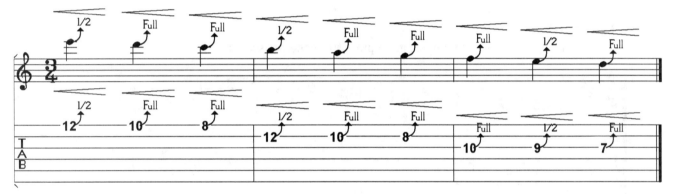

APPLY THIS TECHNIQUE TO EVERY SCALE POSITION, APPLICATION, RHYTHM, AND COMBINATION OF THE FOUR.

5. GHOST PRE BEND AND RELEASE

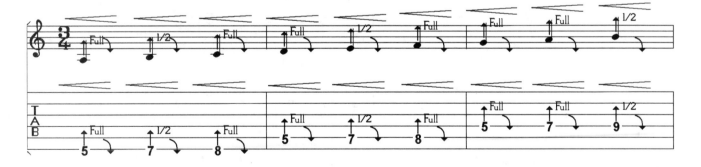

APPLY THIS TECHNIQUE TO EVERY SCALE POSITION, APPLICATION, RHYTHM, AND COMBINATION OF THE FOUR.

CHAPTER 11
DOUBLE NOTE PATTERNS

1. **THIRDS**
   A scale note that is three scale notes up in pitch from another scale note. The 2 notes are played together.

APPLY THIS TO EVERY SCALE POSITION, TECHNIQUE, APPLICATION, RHYTHM, AND COMBINATION OF THE FOUR.

2. **FOURTHS**
   A scale note that is four scale notes up in pitch from another scale note.

APPLY THIS TO EVERY SCALE POSITION, TECHNIQUE, APPLICATION, RHYTHM, AND COMBINATION OF THE FOUR.

3. **FIFTHS**
   A scale note that is five scale notes up in pitch from another scale note.

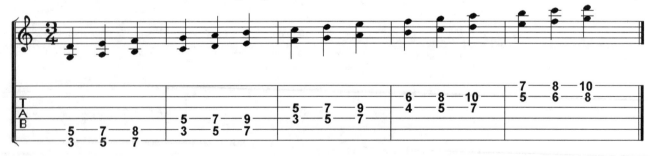

APPLY THIS TO EVERY SCALE POSITION, TECHNIQUE, APPLICATION, RHYTHM, AND COMBINATION OF THE FOUR.

4. SIXTHS 1

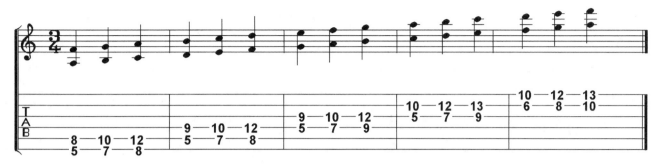

APPLY THIS TO EVERY SCALE POSITION, TECHNIQUE, APPLICATION, RHYTHM, AND
COMBINATION OF THE FOUR.

5. SIXTHS 2

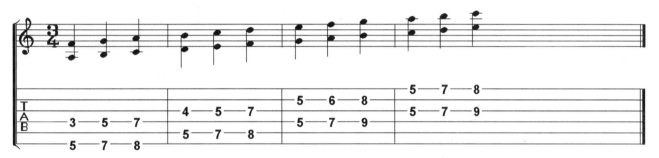

APPLY THIS TO EVERY SCALE POSITION, TECHNIQUE, APPLICATION, RHYTHM, AND
COMBINATION OF THE FOUR.

6. SEVENTHS

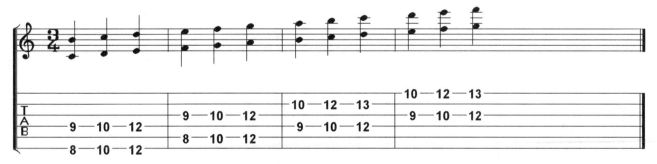

APPLY THIS TO EVERY SCALE POSITION, TECHNIQUE, APPLICATION, RHYTHM, AND
COMBINATION OF THE FOUR.

7. OCTAVES/EIGHTHS 1

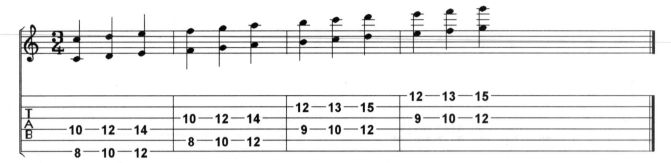

APPLY THIS TO EVERY SCALE POSITION, TECHNIQUE, APPLICATION, RHYTHM, AND
COMBINATION OF THE FOUR.

8. OCTAVES/EIGHTHS 2

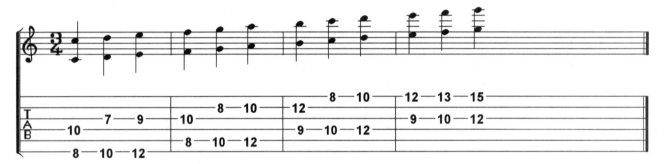

APPLY THIS TO EVERY SCALE POSITION, TECHNIQUE, APPLICATION, RHYTHM, AND
COMBINATION OF THE FOUR.

9. NINTHS/SECONDS

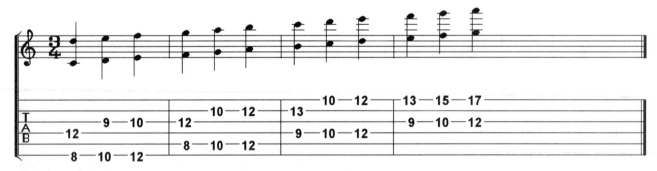

APPLY THIS TO EVERY SCALE POSITION, TECHNIQUE, APPLICATION, RHYTHM, AND
COMBINATION OF THE FOUR.

CHAPTER 12
ADVANCED APPLICATIONS

1. STEP DOWN INC OF III

Play the 3rd scale note, 2nd, 1st. 4th, 3rd, 2nd. 5th, 4th, 3rd. 6th, 5th, 4th. Etc...
This application is written in 3/4 timing.

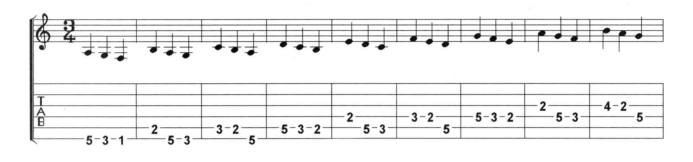

APPLY THIS APPLICATION TO EVERY SCALE POSITION, TECHNIQUE, RHYTHM, AND COMBINATION OF THE FOUR.

2. STEP UP INC OF III

Opposite of step down. 8th scale note, 9th, 10th. 7th, 8th, 9th. 6th, 7th, 8th. Etc...
3/4 timing.

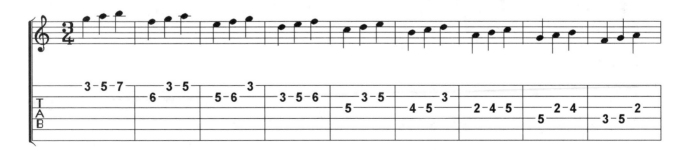

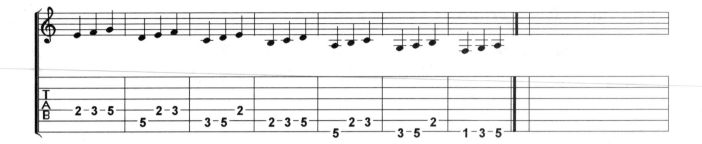

NOW APPLY THIS APPLICATION TO EVERY SCALE POSITION, TECHNIQUE, RHYTHM, AND COMBINATION OF THE FOUR.

3. PIVOT NOTE TO OCTAVE

Play the first scale note, then the second, 1st again, 3rd, 1st, 4th, 1st, 5th, continue this pattern to the octave/8th scale note.

This application is written in 4/4 timing using 16th notes and 8th notes. The count is 1-e-&-a-2-e-&-a-3-e-&-a-4-&/1-e-&-a-2-e-&-a-3-e-&-a-4-&.

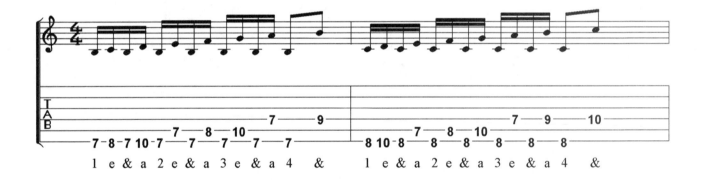

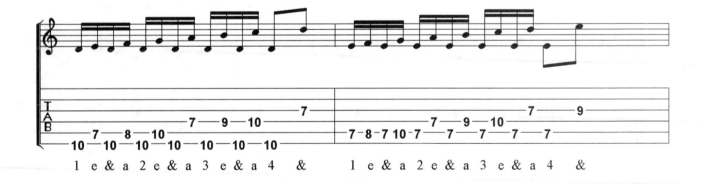

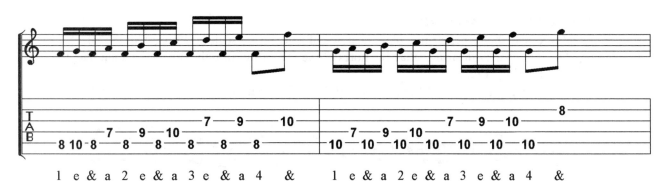

l e & a 2 e & a 3 e & a 4   &   l e & a 2 e & a 3 e & a 4   &

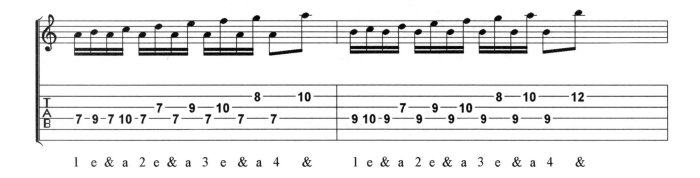

l e & a 2 e & a 3 e & a 4   &   l e & a 2 e & a 3 e & a 4   &

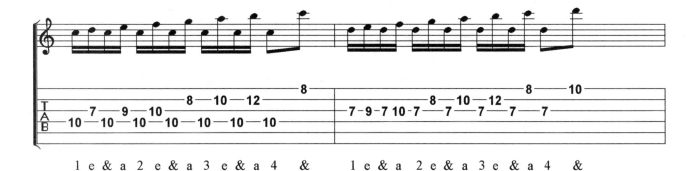

l e & a 2 e & a 3 e & a 4   &   l e & a 2 e & a 3 e & a 4   &

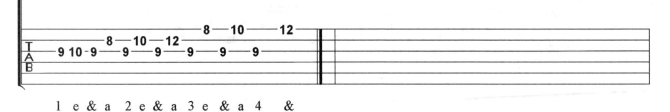

l e & a 2 e & a 3 e & a 4   &

APPLY THIS APPLICATION TO EVERY SCALE POSITION, TECHNIQUE, RHYTHM, AND
COMBINATION OF THE FOUR.

4. TWO STRINGS STRING SKIP

Playing three scale notes per string, play the notes of a 6th string scale position, skip the 5th string, then play the notes of the 4th string. Play the notes of the 5th string, skip the 4th string, then play the notes off the 3rd string. Etc...

This application is written in 2/4 timing using triplets. The count is 1-&-a-2-&-a/1-&-a-2-&-a.

APPLY THIS APPLICATION TO EVERY SCALE POSITION, TECHNIQUE, RHYTHM, AND COMBINATION OF THE FOUR.

5. TWO STRINGS STRING SKIP AND BACK (4 notes)

This application is written in 3/4 timing using 16th and 8th notes. The count is 1-e-&-a-2-e-&-a-3-&/1-e-&-a-2-e-&-a-3-&.

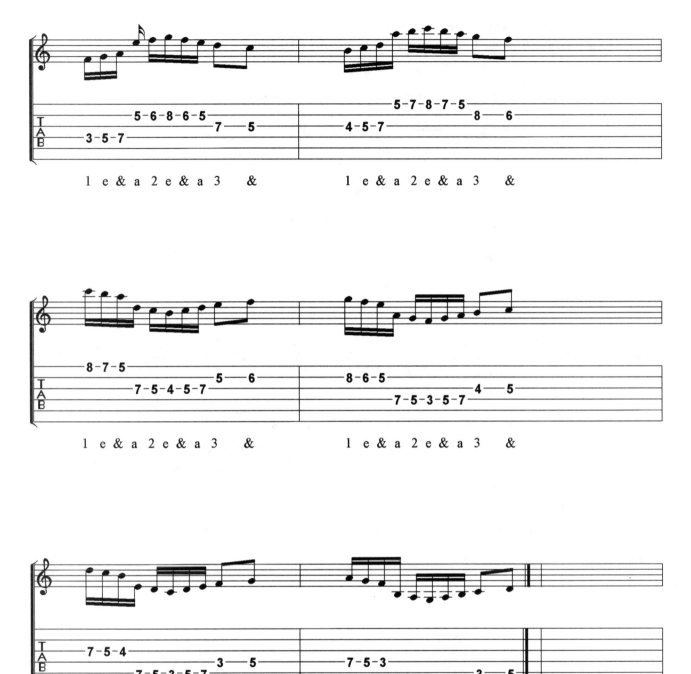

NOW APPLY THIS APPLICATION TO EVERY SCALE POSITION, TECHNIQUE, RHYTHM, AND COMBINATION OF THE FOUR.

6. THREE STRING - STRING SKIP

3/4 timing using triplets. 1-&-a-2-&-a-3-&-a/1-&-a-2-&-a-3-&-a.

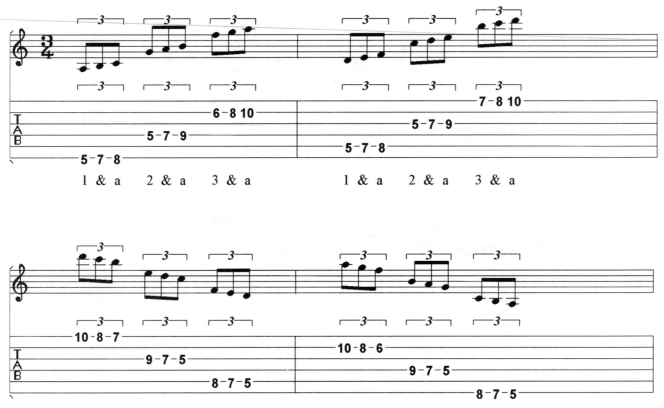

NOW APPLY THIS APPLICATION TO EVERY SCALE POSITION, TECHNIQUE, RHYTHM, AND COMBINATION OF THE FOUR.

7. TWO STRING-STRING SKIP INC OF III

Applying inc. of 3 to string skipping.
3/4 timing using quarter notes. 1-2-3/1-2-3/1-2-3/1-2-3.

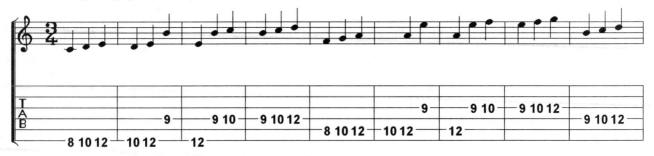

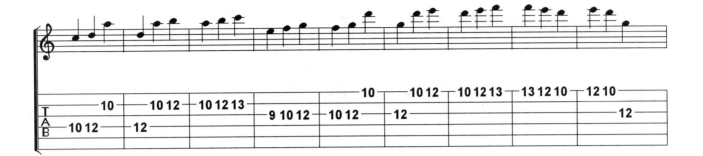

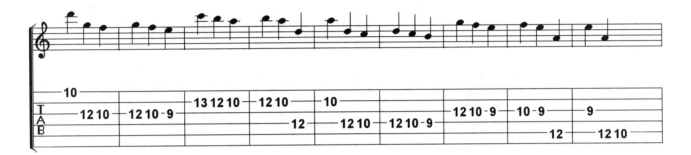

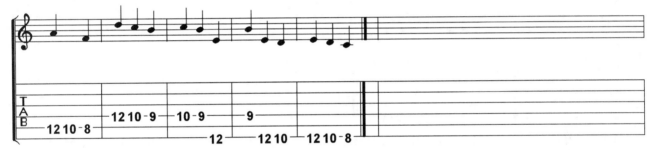

NOW APPLY THIS APPLICATION TO EVERY SCALE POSITION, TECHNIQUE, RHYTHM, AND COMBINATION OF THE FOUR.

8. TWO STRING - STRING SKIP INC OF IV
4/4 timing using quarter notes. 1-2-3-4/1-2-3-4.

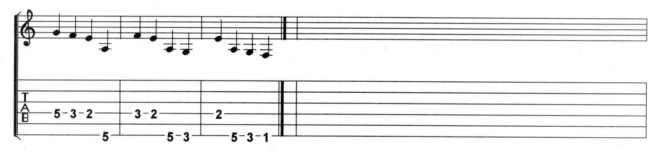

NOW APPLY THIS APPLICATION TO EVERY SCALE POSITION, TECHNIQUE, RHYTHM, AND COMBINATION OF THE FOUR.

MANIAC PATTERNS
9. I-V-III-II-IV-VI-V

Starting with any scale note, count that note as your 1 note, then play the 5th scale note from your one note, then play the 3rd scale note from your 1 note, then 2, 4, 6, then 5.

Application 9, 10, 11, & 12 uses 4/4 timing using 8th notes and quarter notes. 1-&-2-&-3-&-4/1-&-2-&-3-&-4.

APPLY THIS APPLICATION TO EVERY SCALE POSITION, TECHNIQUE, RHYTHM, AND COMBINATION OF THE FOUR.

10. II-IV-VI-VIII-VII-V-IX

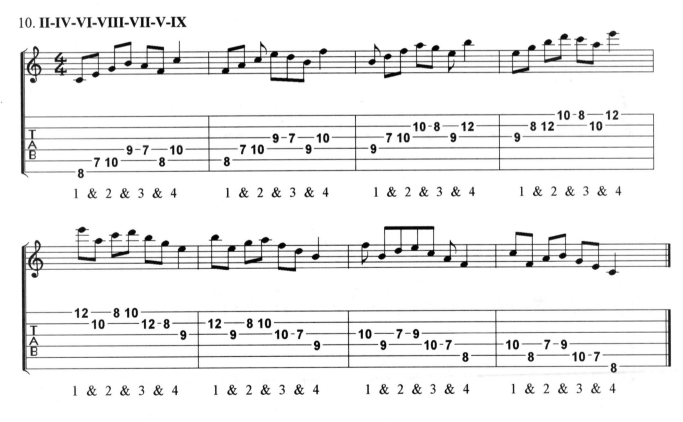

APPLY THIS APPLICATION TO EVERY SCALE POSITION, TECHNIQUE, RHYTHM, AND COMBINATION OF THE FOUR.

11. I-VIII-III-II-VII-IX-VIII

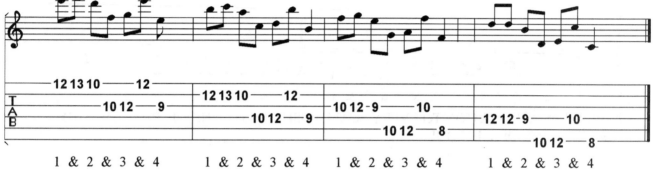

APPLY THIS APPLICATION TO EVERY SCALE POSITION, TECHNIQUE, RHYTHM, AND COMBINATION OF THE FOUR.

12. I-V-IX-VIII-VII-V-III

APPLY THIS APPLICATION TO EVERY SCALE POSITION, TECHNIQUE, RHYTHM, AND COMBINATION OF THE FOUR.

13. TWO STRING - STRING SKIP INC. OF IV & BACK (1 note)
4/4 timing using quarter and 8th notes. 1-2-3-4-&/1-2-3-4-&.

APPLY THIS APPLICATION TO EVERY SCALE POSITION, TECHNIQUE, RHYTHM, AND
COMBINATION OF THE FOUR.

14. TWO STRING - STRING SKIP INC OF IV AND BACK(1 note) IN PATTERNS OF THREE, THEN BACK(3 notes)

4/4 timing using triplets and 8th notes. Notice that the 1st measure is different from the second 1-&-a-2-&-3-&-a-4-&/1-&-2-&-3-&-4-&.

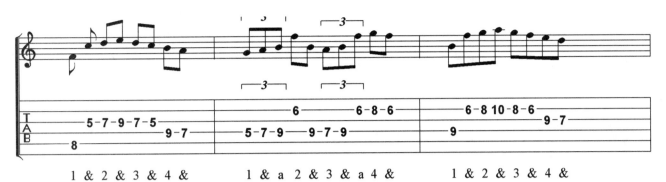

1 & 2 & 3 & 4 &   1 & a 2 & 3 & a 4 &   1 & 2 & 3 & 4 &

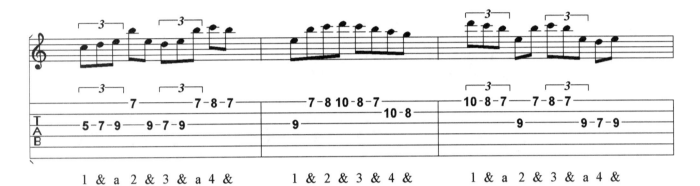

1 & a 2 & 3 & a 4 &   1 & 2 & 3 & 4 &   1 & a 2 & 3 & a 4 &

1 & 2 & 3 & 4 &   1 & a 2 & 3 & a 4 &   1 & 2 & 3 & 4 &

1 & a 2 & 3 & a 4 &   1 & 2 & 3 & 4 &   1 & a 2 & 3 & a 4 &

1 & 2 & 3 & 4 &

APPLY THIS APPLICATION TO EVERY SCALE POSITION, TECHNIQUE, RHYTHM, AND
COMBINATION OF THE FOUR.

15. STEP DOWN/STEP UP INC OF III PATTERNS OF THREE
3/4 timing using triplets. 1-&-a-2-&-a-3-&-a/1-&-a-2-&-a-3-&-a.
STEP DOWN

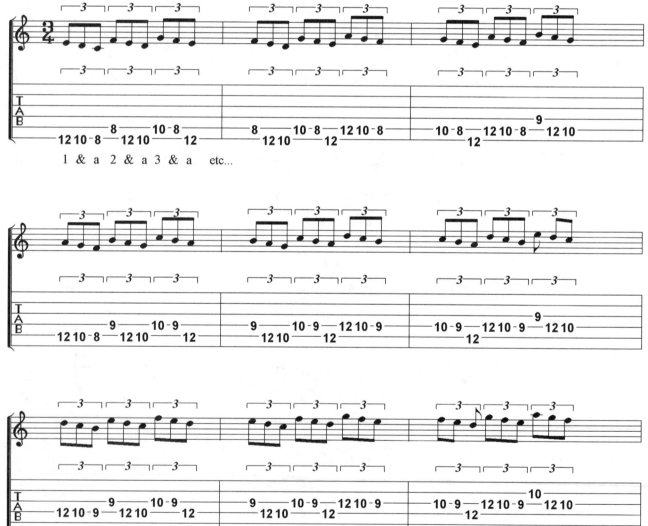

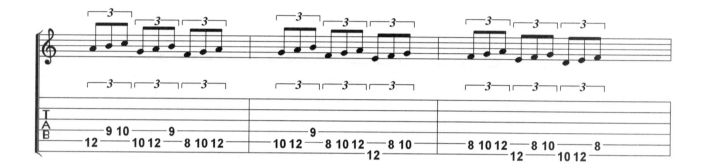

APPLY THIS APPLICATION TO EVERY SCALE POSITION, TECHNIQUE, RHYTHM, AND COMBINATION OF THE FOUR.

16. INC OF III PATTERNS OF FOUR

4/4 timing using triplets. 1-&-a-2-&-a-3-&-a-4-&-a/1-&-a-2-&-a-3-&-a-4-&-a.

1 & a 2 & a 3 & a 4 & a   etc...

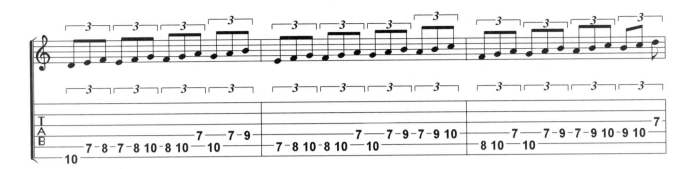

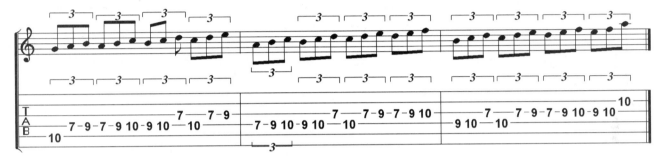

APPLY THIS APPLICATION TO EVERY SCALE POSITION, TECHNIQUE, RHYTHM, AND COMBINATION OF THE FOUR.

17. INC OF IV PATTERNS OF THREE

3/4 timing using 16th notes.   1-e-&-a-2-e-&-a-3-e-&-a/1-e-&-a-2-e-&-a-3-e-&-a.

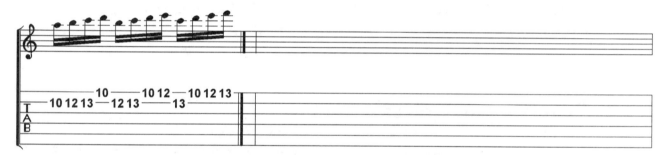

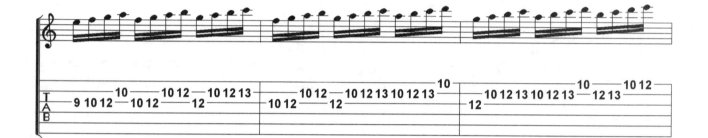

APPLY THIS APPLICATION TO EVERY SCALE POSITION, TECHNIQUE, RHYTHM, AND COMBINATION OF THE FOUR.

18. STEP DOWN STEP UP PATTERNS OF FOUR

4/4 timing using 8th notes. 1-&-2-&-3-&-4-&/1-&-2-&-3-&-4-&.

STEP DOWN

APPLY THIS APPLICATION TO EVERY SCALE POSITION, TECHNIQUE, RHYTHM, AND COMBINATION OF THE FOUR.

STEP UP

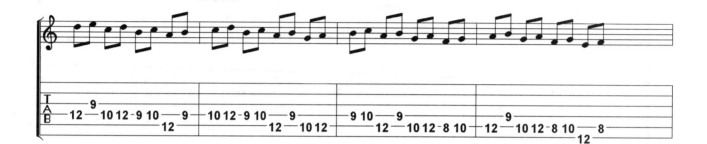

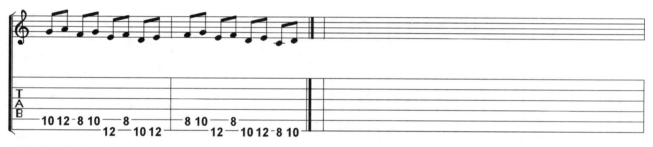

APPLY THIS APPLICATION TO EVERY SCALE POSITION, TECHNIQUE, RHYTHM, AND COMBINATION OF THE FOUR.

19. INC OF II PATTERNS OF FOUR

4/4 timing using 8th notes. 1-&-2-&-3-&-4-&/1-&-2-&-3-&-4-&.

1 & 2 & 3 & 4 & etc...

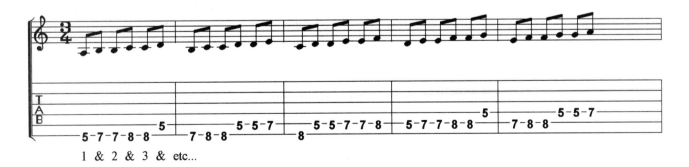

APPLY THIS APPLICATION TO EVERY SCALE POSITION, TECHNIQUE, RHYTHM, AND COMBINATION OF THE FOUR.

20. INC OF II PATTERNS OF THREE

3/4 timing using 8th notes. 1-&-2-&-3-&/1-&-2-&-3-&.

1 & 2 & 3 & etc...

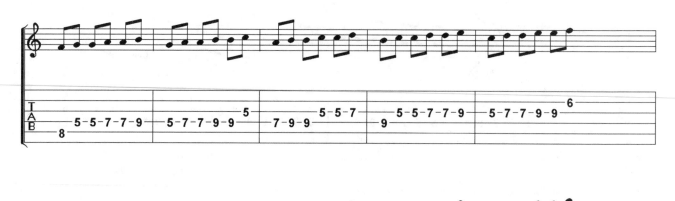

APPLY THIS APPLICATION TO EVERY SCALE POSITION, TECHNIQUE, RHYTHM, AND
COMBINATION OF THE FOUR.

Congratulations! If you have followed this coarse from page one, you have achieved a great
playing ability as well as a great level of knowledge on your guitar. If you haven't already
exhausted yourself trying all the techniques and applications in every scale position, I suggest that
you do so. Throughout this book I have left constant reminders after each piece:

APPLY THIS APPLICATION TO EVERY SCALE POSITION, TECHNIQUE, RHYTHM, AND COMBINATION
OF THE FOUR.

To some it may seem redundant, but I include the reminder for a reason. Each and every new
technique or application you learn can be explored for a lifetime. There is no limit. When you
push yourself and your limits, you will broaden your horizons. That is how new styles of playing
have been created. That is what makes a player one of the "greats". If you are dedicated to music,
in this case guitar, you will greatly benefit by playing these pieces, not only in the positions I have
written them in, but also in the other scale positions you have learned, and later to the other keys
and scales in the remainder of this book. I also recommend using your own creativity to come up
with your own combinations of notes, techniques, applications, and rhythms. Once again, pushing
your limits will broaden your capabilities and make you a better guitarist. This applies to anything
in life.

CHAPTER 13
MODES, OTHER VARIATIONS OF THE NATURAL SCALE

The natural scale, as we know, consists of the major and minor key. It also consists of 5 others. Just as there are 7 notes in the natural scale, there are 7 modes as well. They are Aeolian, Locrian, Ionian, Dorian, Phrygian, Lydian, and Mixolydian. A mode is another name for a scale. When playing the natural scale we know if our focus is on the A note, or in other words, we make A our root note, we are playing the minor scale. Technically this natural scale A to A is called the Aeolian mode. Here is a list of each mode in the natural scale:

The natural scale A to A is called the Aeolian mode. A-B-C-D-E-F-G-A-ETC...
The natural scale B to B is called the Locrian mode. B-C-D-E-F-G-A-B-ETC...
The natural scale C to C is called the Ionian mode. C-D-E-F-G-A-B-C-ETC...
The natural scale D to D is called the Dorian mode. D-E-F-G-A-B-C-D-ETC...
The natural scale E to E is called the Phrygian mode. E-F-G-A-B-C-D-E-ETC...
The natural scale F to F is called the Lydian mode. F-G-A-B-C-D-E-F-ETC...
The natural scale G to G is called the Mixolydian mode. G-A-B-C-D-E-F-G-ETC...

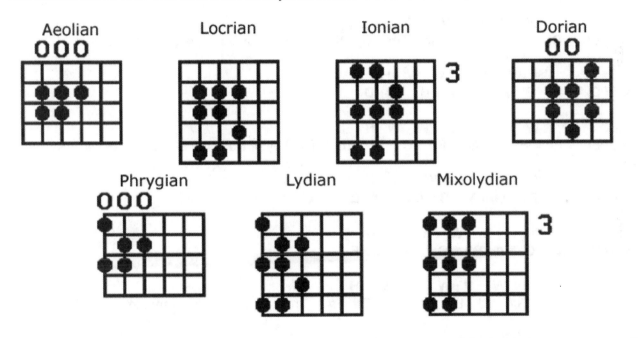

These are technical definitions. That is why I saved them for this part of the book. In one sentence it can be summed up to this; All seven modes equal one natural scale. You have been playing all seven modes since the beginning of this book. We will learn more on modes after we learn to change keys.

CHAPTER 14
KEY CHANGES AND SCALE PATTERNS

When someone refers to the key of C, they are referring to the natural scale or C major/Ionian scale. When someone refers to the key of A, they are referring to the key of A major/Ionian. The key of A major is the C to C natural scale <u>pattern</u> applied to the A note as the root.

Distance between notes can be measured by whole steps and half steps. A whole step is equal to two frets on the guitar. A half step is equal to one fret. When you want to change the key of a scale/song just apply the same pattern of whole steps and half steps to the key you wish to play in.

EXAMPLE: The C natural, major scale from root to root is made of a whole step, whole step, half step, whole step, whole step, whole step, half step. The sixth note of each major scale is the minor root note, also known as the Relative Minor.

Universal Major Scale Formula
W = Whole Step
H = Half Step

```
W   W   H   W   W   W   H
1   2   3   4   5   6   7   1
```

Any major scale, regardless of what key it is: A, B, C, D etc..., will apply to this major scale formula: whole step, whole step, half step, whole step, whole step, whole step, half step

The examples below show each key of the musical alphabet. Notice that they all have the same major scale formula applied.

```
                W  W  H  W  W  W  H
Key of C     C  D  E  F  G  A  B  C
```

```
                  W  W  H  W  W  W  H
Key of Db    Db Eb  F  Gb Ab Bb  C  Db    The key of Db is the same key as C#
```

```
                 W  W  H  W  W  W  H
Key of D     D  E  F# G  A  B  C# D
```

```
                W  W  H  W  W  W  H
Key of Eb    Eb  F  G  Ab Bb  C  D  Eb    The key of Eb is the same key as D#
```

```
                W  W  H  W  W  W  H
Key of E     E  F# G# A  B  C# D# E
```

```
                W  W  H  W  W  W  H
Key of F     F  G  A  Bb C  D  E  F
```

```
                W  W  H  W  W  W  H
Key of F#    F#  G# A# B  C# D# E# F#    The key of F# is the same key as Gb
```

```
                W  W  H  W  W  W  H
Key of G     G  A  B  C  D  E  F# G
```

```
                W  W  H  W  W  W  H
Key of Ab    Ab Bb  C  Db Eb  F  G  Ab    The key of Ab is the same key as G#
```

```
                W  W  H  W  W  W  H
Key of A     A  B  C# D  E  F# G# A
```

```
                W  W  H  W  W  W  H
Key of Bb    Bb  C  D  Eb  F  G  A  Bb    The key of Bb is the same key as A#
```

```
                W  W  H  W  W  W  H
Key of B     B  C# D# E  F# G# A# B
```

CHAPTER 15
THE KEY OF A MAJOR, F# MINOR

The following 11 chapters will feature charts and notation for each key of music. To achieve total mastery of the guitar, apply your favorite techniques, applications, and rhythms to each key.

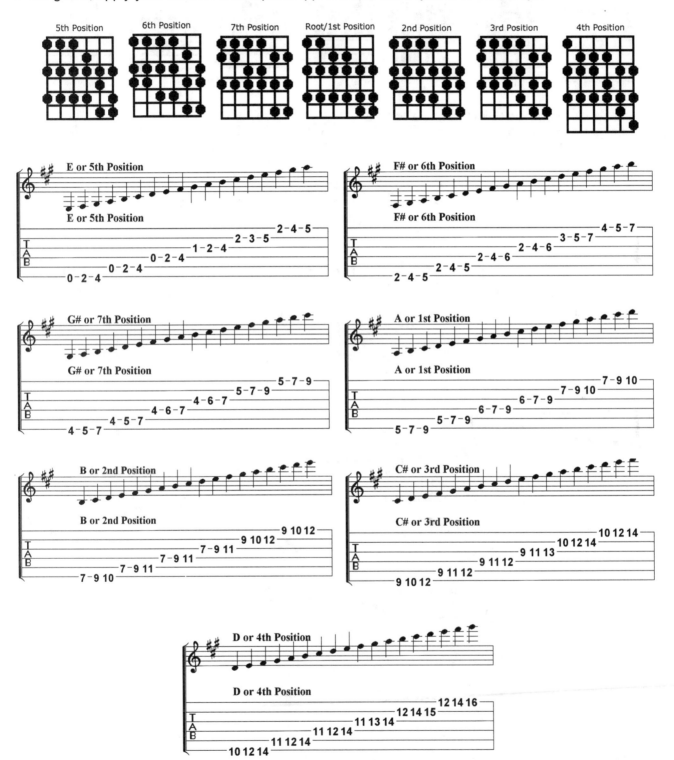

CHAPTER 16
THE KEY OF Bb MAJOR, G MINOR

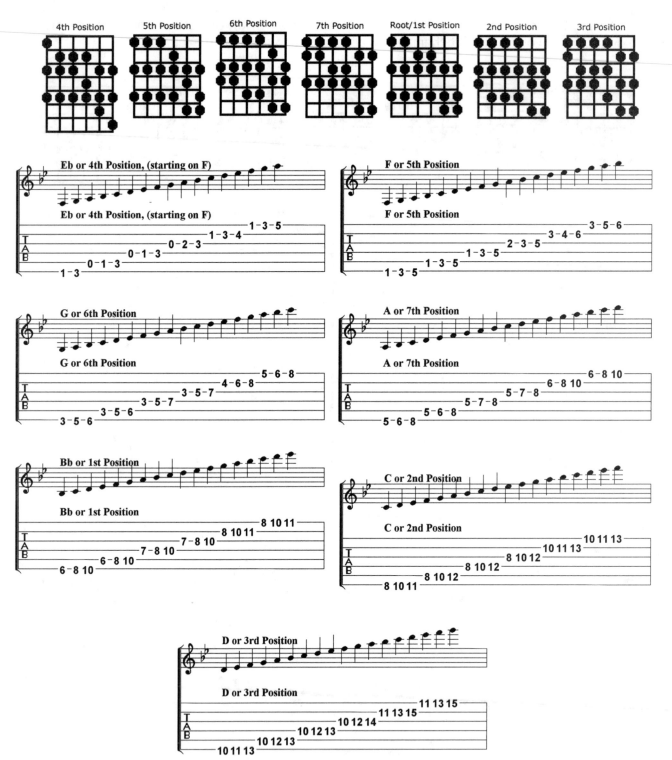

CHAPTER 17
THE KEY OF B MAJOR, G# MINOR

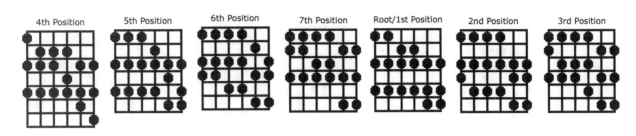

4th Position   5th Position   6th Position   7th Position   Root/1st Position   2nd Position   3rd Position

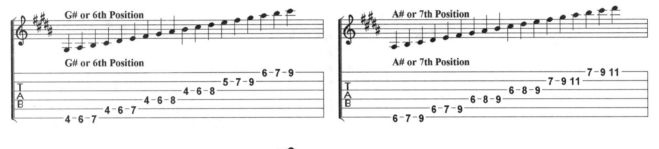

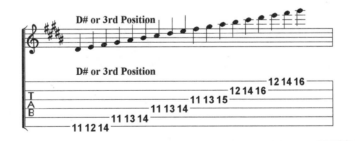

CHAPTER 18
THE KEY OF Db MAJOR, Bb MINOR

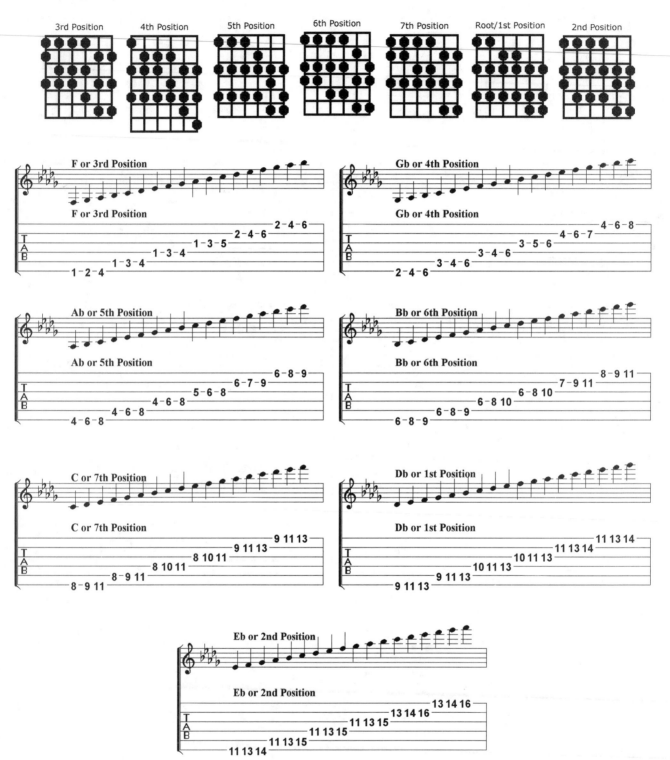

CHAPTER 19
THE KEY OF D MAJOR, B MINOR

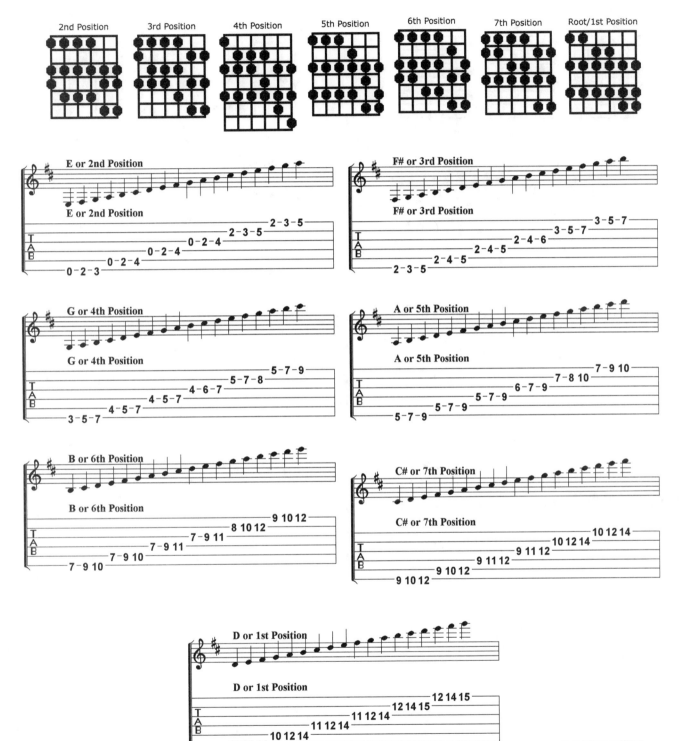

CHAPTER 20
THE KEY OF Eb MAJOR, C MINOR

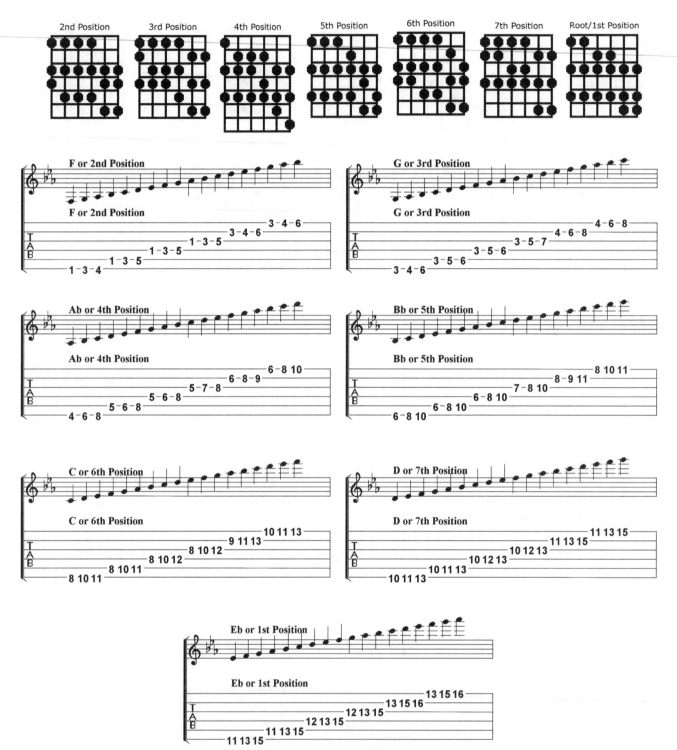

CHAPTER 21
THE KEY OF E MAJOR, C# MINOR

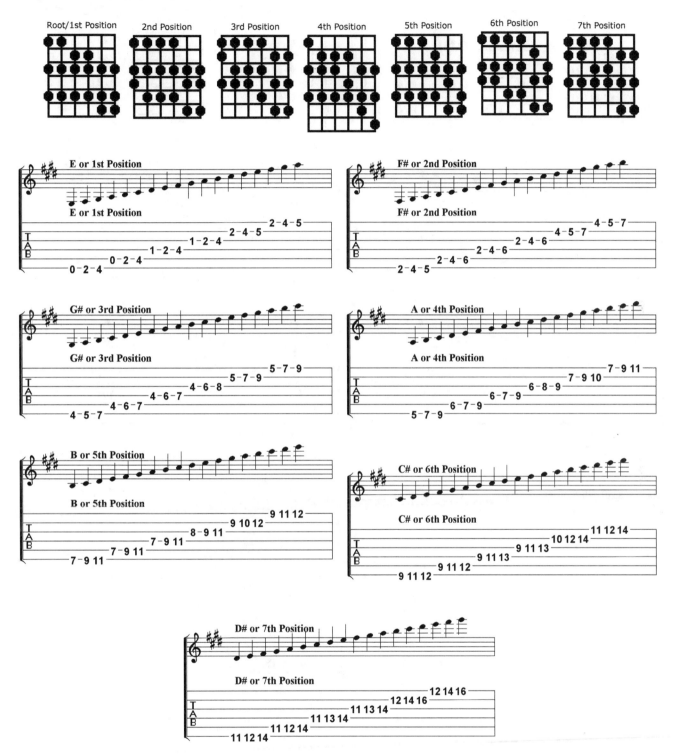

CHAPTER 22
THE KEY OF F MAJOR, D MINOR

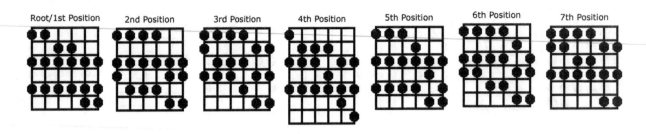

Root/1st Position   2nd Position   3rd Position   4th Position   5th Position   6th Position   7th Position

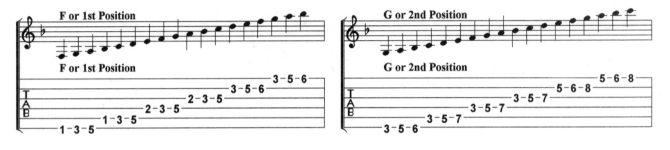

F or 1st Position

F or 1st Position
```
                                    3 - 5 - 6
                            3 - 5 - 6
                    2 - 3 - 5
                1 - 3 - 5
            2 - 3 - 5
        1 - 3 - 5
```

G or 2nd Position

G or 2nd Position
```
                                    5 - 6 - 8
                            5 - 6 - 8
                    3 - 5 - 7
                3 - 5 - 7
            3 - 5 - 7
        3 - 5 - 6
```

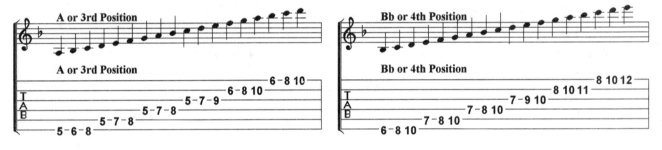

A or 3rd Position

A or 3rd Position
```
                                    6 - 8 10
                            6 - 8 10
                    5 - 7 - 9
                5 - 7 - 8
            5 - 7 - 8
        5 - 6 - 8
```

Bb or 4th Position

Bb or 4th Position
```
                                    8 10 12
                            8 10 11
                    7 - 9 10
                7 - 8 10
            7 - 8 10
        6 - 8 10
```

C or 5th Position

C or 5th Position
```
                                    10 12 13
                            10 11 13
                    9 10 12
                8 10 12
            8 10 12
        8 10 12
```

D or 6th Position

D or 6th Position
```
                                    12 13 15
                            11 13 15
                    10 12 14
                10 12 14
            10 12 13
        10 12 13
```

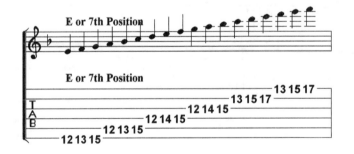

E or 7th Position

E or 7th Position
```
                                    13 15 17
                            13 15 17
                    12 14 15
                12 14 15
            12 13 15
        12 13 15
```

CHAPTER 23
THE KEY OF F# MAJOR, D# MINOR

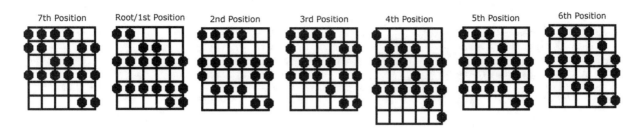

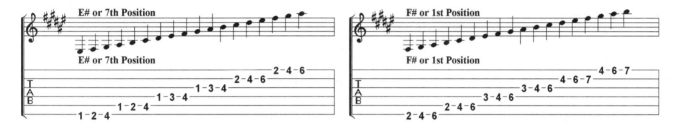

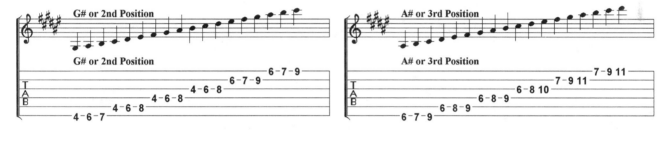

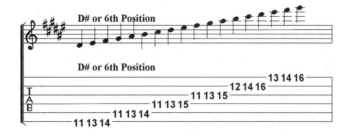

CHAPTER 24
THE KEY OF G MAJOR, E MINOR

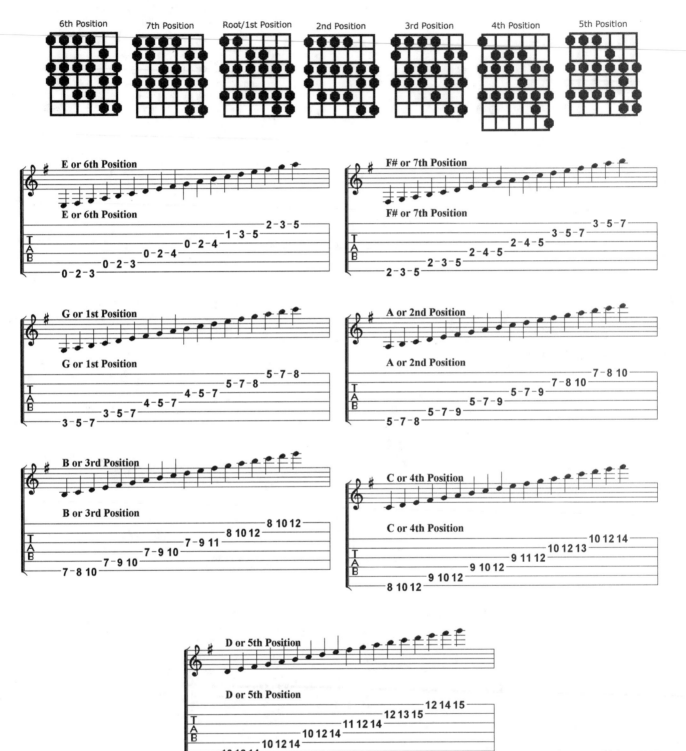

CHAPTER 25
THE KEY OF Ab MAJOR, F MINOR

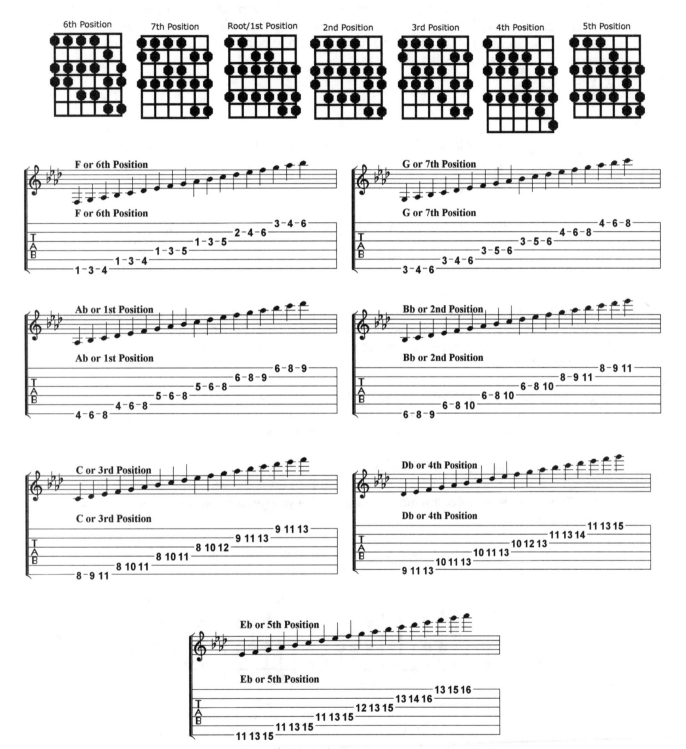

CHAPTER 26
SCALES AS MODES IN DIFFERENT KEYS

You now know the Ionian (major), Dorian, Phrygian, Lydian, Mixolydian, Aeolian (minor), and Locrian scales/modes in every key, and every position on the guitar. Also, these modes derive from the natural scale patterns. So when you convert the natural scale to numbers or scale degrees you can then covert the modes to fit the key you wish to play in.

```
C D E F G A B C
1 2 3 4 5 6 7 8/1
```

FOR EXAMPLE: When you are playing the natural scale D to D (2 to 2) you are playing the Dorian mode.

```
C D E F G A B C D
1 2 3 4 5 6 7 8/1 2
```

If you change to the key of G and play A to A (2 to 2) you are also playing the Dorian mode.

```
G A B C D E F# G A
1 2 3 4 5 6 7 8/1 2
```

If you don't understand the study of modes, don't worry much. Knowledge of modes is not necessary to play great guitar. At this point you know the scales that encompass all modes! You know the major and minor root notes, and many techniques, applications, and rhythms. These are the important tools for being a great player.

Try experimenting with different modes in place of the major or minor scales. For example, you might like the sound of **A** Dorian over an **A** minor chord. Or, since the F chord is made up of F-**A**-C, try an **A** Dorian mode over F. Since **C** is a part of the F chord, try **C** Locrian.

You can also mix these up in a rhythm progression. One measure you might go from the **F** chord to an **F** major run. The next measure you might go from **F** to an **A** Dorian run. Then from the **F** chord to a **C** Dorian run. Experiment with all of the modes. Then, once you get familiar with what works best for you, mix in your favorite techniques and applications.

Below is a chart of all 7 modes played from root to octave, beginning on the 5th string. To play these in the key of C, start each mode on the third fret of the 5th string.

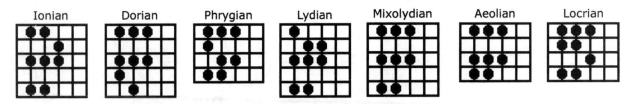

While modes can really enhance your playing style, don't worry too much if you don't grasp the concept right away. I've witnessed many guitarists dive head first into the study of modes, only to forget the big picture of why the started playing guitar in the first place...
...to make music, and have fun doing it.

See MODE CHARTS and ADVANCED LEAD GUITAR CONCEPTS in the bonus section on page 167.

OTHER SCALES

There are many more scales than what we have learned so far. The remainder of this book will contain several scales from many different countries and cultures. Be aware of the similarities and differences. Try combining these scales to others. You may find it is pleasant to hear a key change or scale change during a song or solo.

CHAPTER 27
THE PENTATONIC SCALE

Known widely as the Blues or Rock scale, the Pentatonic scale consists of the same notes as the natural scale, less the 4th and 7th scale degrees.

Major Pentatonic

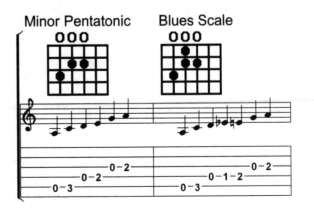

C	D	E	F	G	A	B	C
1	2	3	4	5	6	7	8/1

The step pattern for the pentatonic scale is WHOLE, WHOLE, ONE AND ONE HALF, WHOLE, ONE AND A HALF or W - W - W/H - W - W/H. Applied to the C note it looks like this:

W	W	W/H	W	W/H
C	D	E	G	A	C

THE MINOR PENTATONIC / BLUES SCALE

Just like the natural scale, use the C note as your root for the major pentatonic scale. For the minor pentatonic scale use the A note as your root.

For reference, the minor pentatonic scale pattern is ONE AND A HALF, WHOLE, WHOLE, ONE AND A HALF, WHOLE. Applied to an A note it looks like this:

W/H	W	W	W/H	W
A	C	D	E	G	A

The minor pentatonic scale is used mostly for blues. Some methods will teach you that the Blues Scale is the Pentatonic adding a $b5^{th}$ note. Personally, I consider the $b5^{th}$ note a passing tone. You can learn the scale both ways if you wish.

Minor Pentatonic   Blues Scale

KEY OF C MAJOR, A MINOR PENTATONIC

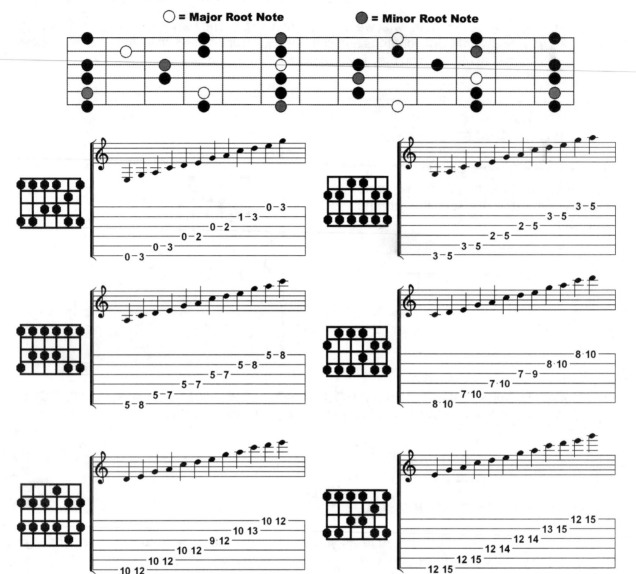

Since the Pentatonic scale is so widely used in popular music, it is highly recommended that you combine the different positions of the pentatonic scale with some of the techniques and applications we have learned so far throughout this course. In one way, this will test your memory of all the tricks and techniques we've learned so far, and it will also act as an example of how you can apply tricks and techniques to the exotic and cultural scales to come.

EXOTIC SCALES

Many of these scales come from different cultures around the world. While there is no standard form of theory or practice in using them in popular musical styles, they still find their way into the mainstream often. When exploring these scales, try adding them to songs and progressions you already play. While they may not work all of the time, you will find some amazing phrases to add to your guitar playing.

At this stage you should be comfortable with changing keys and applying techniques and applications to these exotic scales. If you do need the extra guidance required to take these exotic scales a step further, please visit MJSPublications.com/moretsta.php. There you will find updates about products that will continue your guitar training using the Total Scales Techniques and Applications method beyond the scope of this course.

CHAPTER 28
THE ARABIAN SCALE

The step pattern for the Arabian scale is W-W-H-H-W-W-W. Applied to the C note it looks like this:

W	W	H	H	W	W	W
C	D	E	F	Gb	Ab	Bb	C

KEY OF C ARABIAN

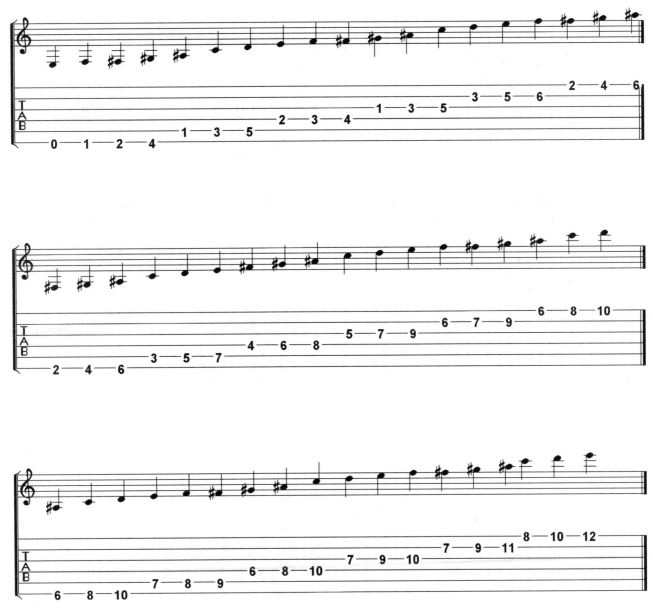

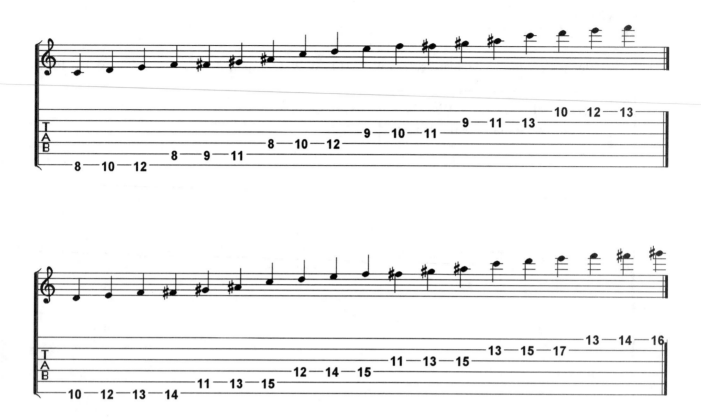

NOW APPLY THIS SCALE TO EVERY KEY, TECHNIQUE, APPLICATION, RHYTHM, AND COMBINATION OF THE FOUR.

CHAPTER 29
THE BALINESE SCALE
FORMULA: H W WW H WW
APPLIED TO C

H	W	WW	H	WW	
C	Db	Eb	G	Ab	C

KEY OF C BALINESE

NOW APPLY THIS SCALE TO EVERY KEY, TECHNIQUE, APPLICATION, RHYTHM, AND COMBINATION OF THE FOUR.

CHAPTER 30
THE BOP SCALE
FORMULA: H W H W H W H W
APPLIED TO C

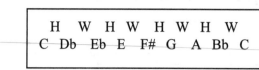

H	W	H	W	H	W	H	W
C	Db	Eb	E	F#	G	A	Bb	C

KEY OF C BOP

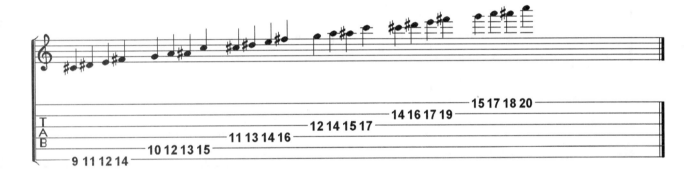

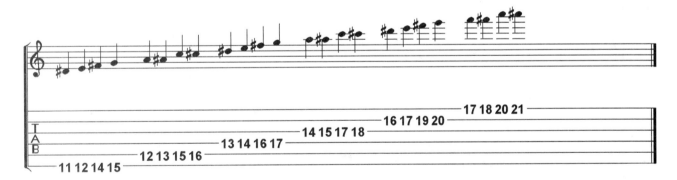

NOW APPLY THIS SCALE TO EVERY KEY, TECHNIQUE, APPLICATION, RHYTHM, AND COMBINATION OF THE FOUR.

CHAPTER 31
THE DIMINISHED SCALE
FORMULA: W H W H W H W H

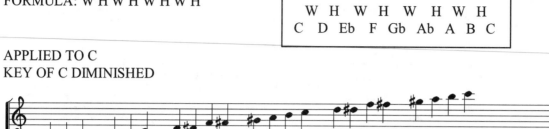

W		H		W		H		W		H		W		H
C		D		Eb		F		Gb		Ab		A		B	C

APPLIED TO C
KEY OF C DIMINISHED

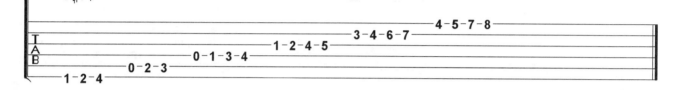

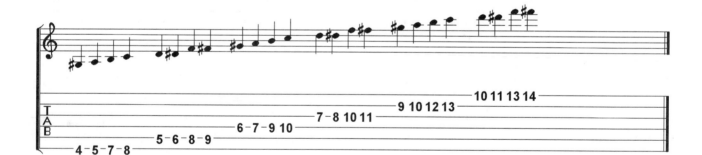

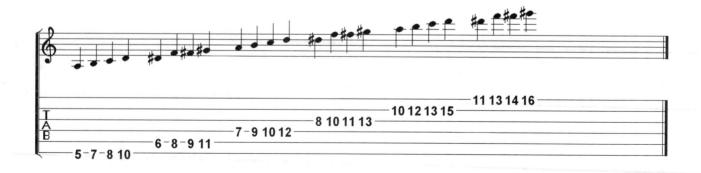

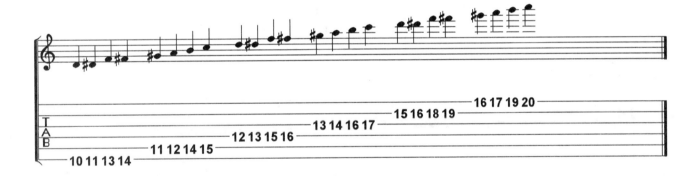

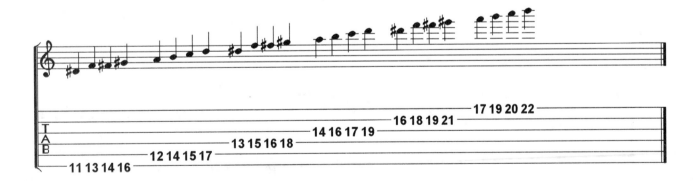

Another way to play the F form

NOW APPLY THIS SCALE TO EVERY KEY, TECHNIQUE, APPLICATION, RHYTHM, AND COMBINATION OF THE FOUR.

CHAPTER 32
THE DOMINANT 7,b5 SCALE
FORMULA: W W H H WH H W

APPLIED TO C

W	W	H	H	WH	H	W	
C	D	E	F	Gb		A	Bb	C

KEY OF C DOMINANT 7,b5

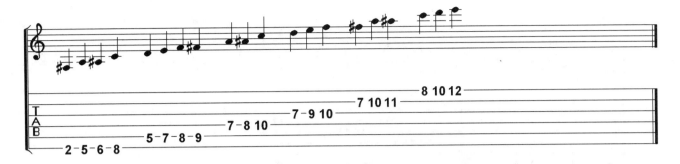

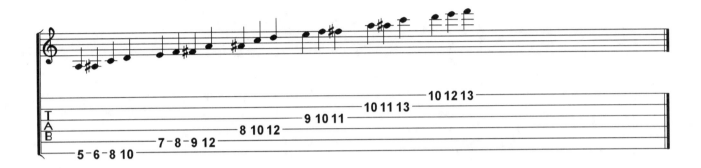

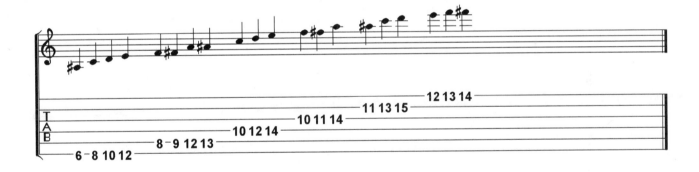

Another way to play the E form

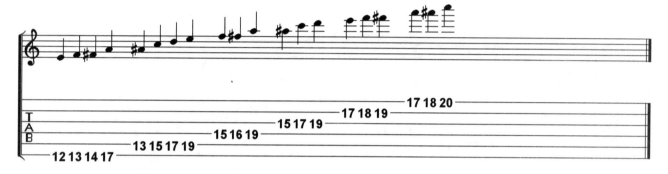

NOW APPLY THIS SCALE TO EVERY KEY, TECHNIQUE, APPLICATION, RHYTHM, AND COMBINATION OF THE FOUR.

CHAPTER 33
THE DOMINANT 7,b9 SCALE
FORMULA: H WH H H W H W
APPLIED TO C

H	WH	H	H	W	H	W
C	Db	E	F	G	A	Bb	C

KEY OF C DOMINANT 7,b9

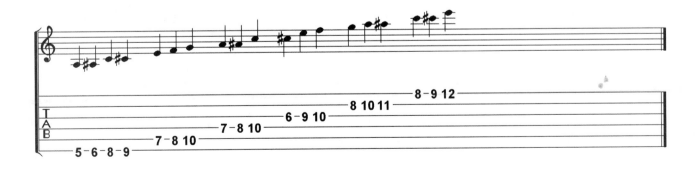

NOW APPLY THIS SCALE TO EVERY KEY, TECHNIQUE, APPLICATION, RHYTHM, AND COMBINATION OF THE FOUR.

CHAPTER 34
THE DOMINANT 7,b9,#11 SCALE
FORMULA: H WH W H W H W
APPLIED TO C

H	WH W	H W H	W
C Db	E	F# G	A Bb C

KEY OF C DOMINANT 7, b9, #11

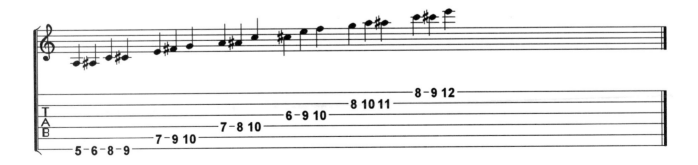

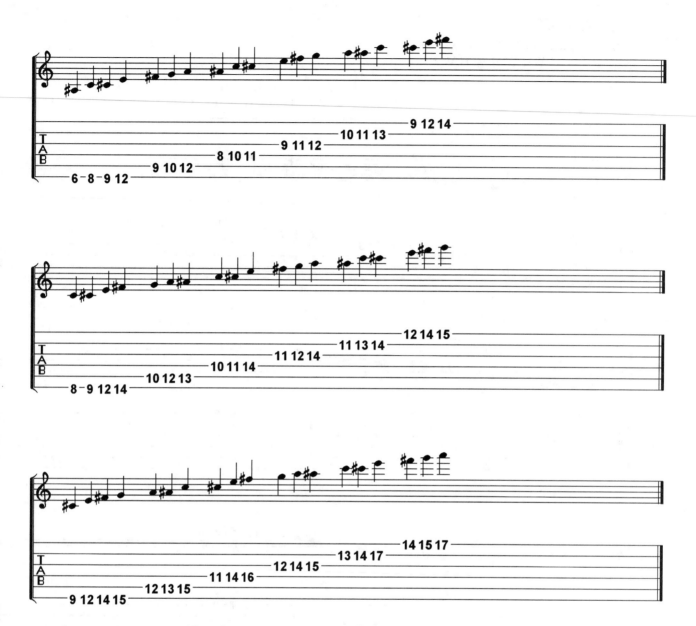

NOW APPLY THIS SCALE TO EVERY KEY, TECHNIQUE, APPLICATION, RHYTHM, AND COMBINATION OF THE FOUR.

119

CHAPTER 35
THE DOMINANT 7, #9 SCALE
FORMULA: WH H H W W H W
APPLIED TO C

WH	H	H	W	W	H	W
C	D#	E	F	G	A	Bb	C

KEY OF C DOMINANT 7, #9

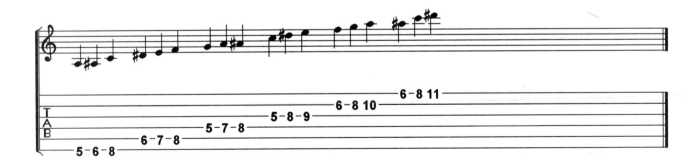

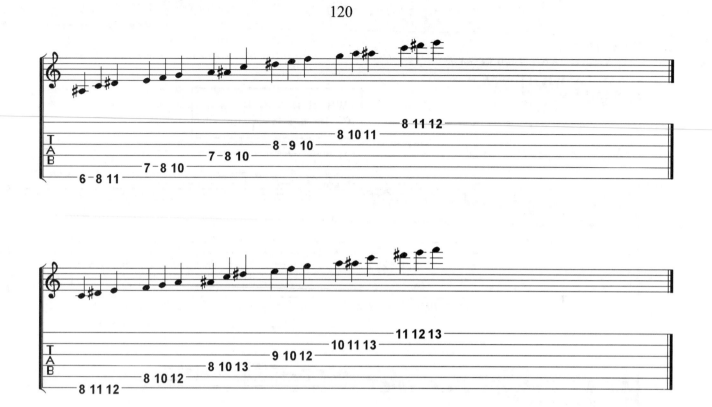

NOW APPLY THIS SCALE TO EVERY KEY, TECHNIQUE, APPLICATION, RHYTHM, AND
COMBINATION OF THE FOUR.

CHAPTER 36
THE DOMINANT 7, #5, #9, #11 SCALE
FORMULA: WH H W W W H H W
APPLIED TO C

WH		H	W	W	H	H	W
C	D#	E	F#	G#	A	Bb	C

KEY OF C DOMINANT 7, #5, #9, #11

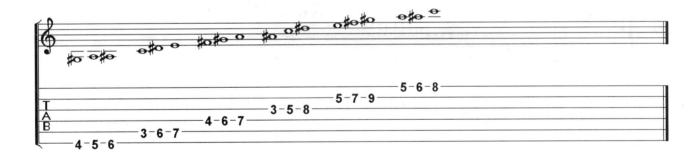

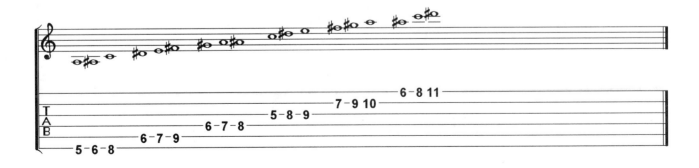

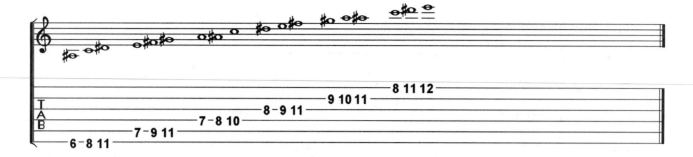

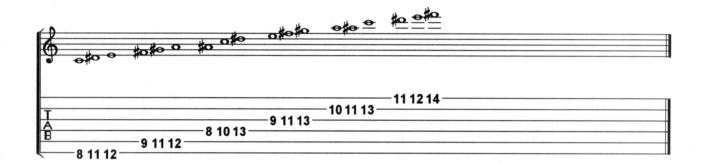

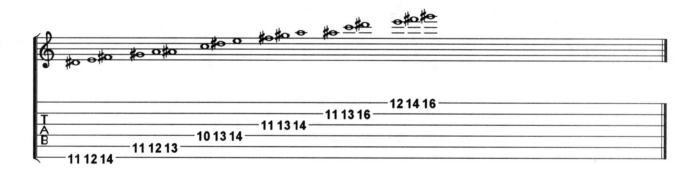

NOW APPLY THIS SCALE TO EVERY KEY, TECHNIQUE, APPLICATION, RHYTHM, AND COMBINATION OF THE FOUR.

CHAPTER 37
THE DOMINANT 9, #11 SCALE
FORMULA: W W W H W H W

APPLIED TO C

W	W	W	H	W	H	W
C	D	E	F#	G	A	Bb	C

KEY OF C DOMINANT 9, #11

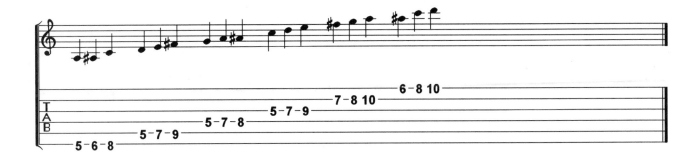

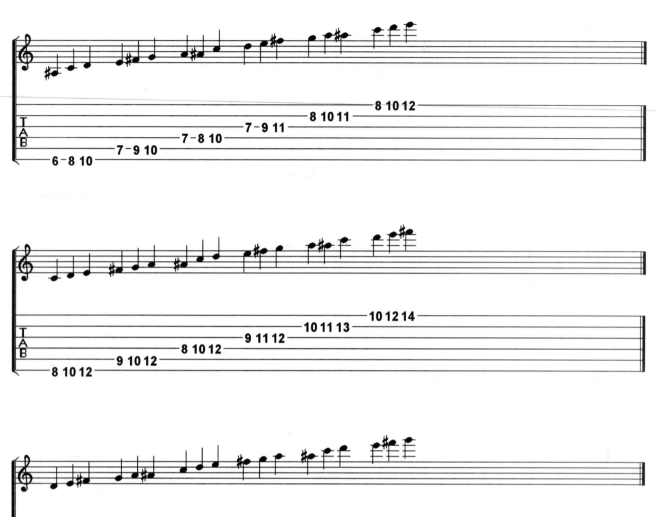

APPLY THIS SCALE TO EVERY KEY, TECHNIQUE, APPLICATION, RHYTHM, AND COMBINATION OF THE FOUR.

CHAPTER 38
THE HARMONIC MINOR SCALE
FORMULA: W H W W H WH H
APPLIED TO C

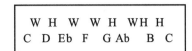

KEY OF C HARMONIC MINOR

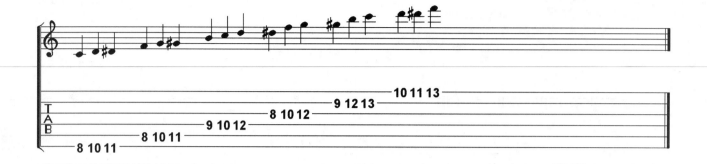

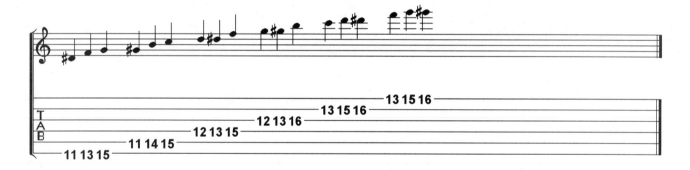

NOW APPLY THIS SCALE TO EVERY KEY, TECHNIQUE, APPLICATION, RHYTHM, AND COMBINATION OF THE FOUR.

CHAPTER 39
THE HAWAIIAN SCALE
FORMULA: W H W W W W H
APPLIED TO C

KEY OF C HAWAIIAN

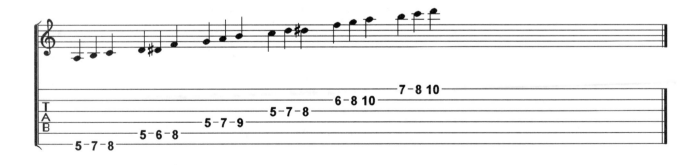

128

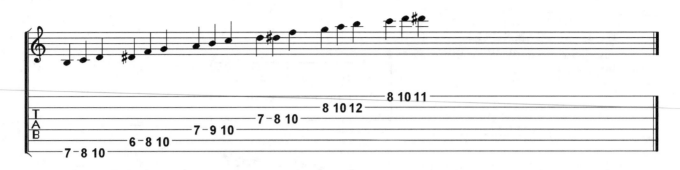

NOW APPLY THIS SCALE TO EVERY KEY, TECHNIQUE, APPLICATION, RHYTHM, AND COMBINATION OF THE FOUR.

CHAPTER 40
THE HUNGARIAN GYPSY SCALE
FORMULA: H WH H W H WH H
APPLIED TO C

H	WH	H	W	H	WH	H
C	Db	E	F	G	Ab	B C

KEY OF C HUNGARIAN GYPSY

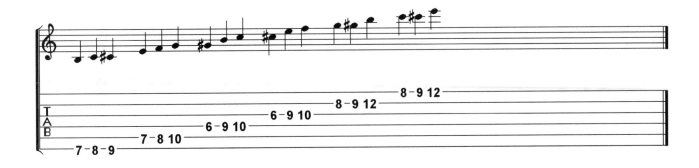

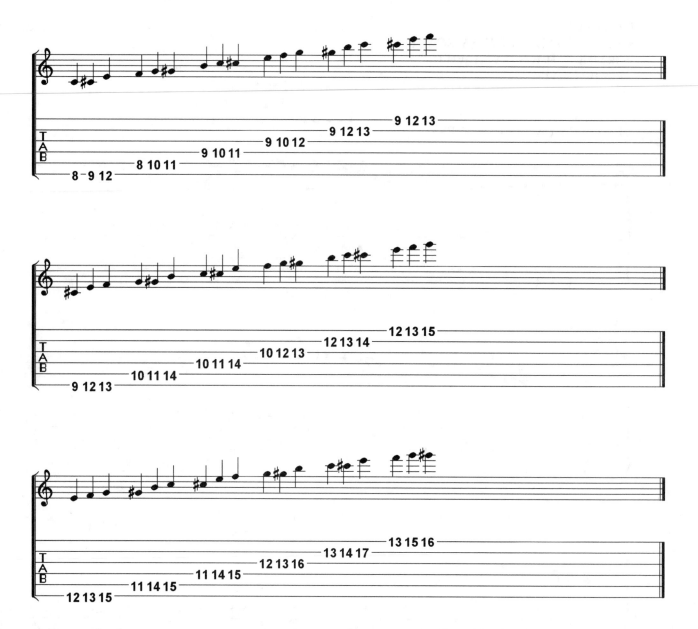

NOW APPLY THIS SCALE TO EVERY KEY, TECHNIQUE, APPLICATION, RHYTHM, AND COMBINATION OF THE FOUR.

CHAPTER 41
THE HUNGARIAN MAJOR SCALE
FORMULA: WH H W H W H W
APPLIED TO C

WH		H	W		H	W		H	W	
C		D#	E		F#	G		A	Bb	C

KEY OF C HUNGARIAN MAJOR

132

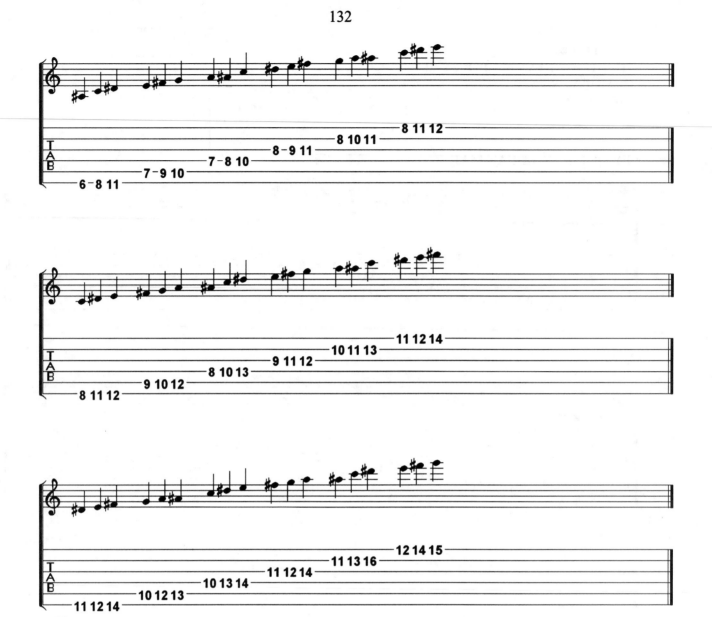

NOW APPLY THIS SCALE TO EVERY KEY, TECHNIQUE, APPLICATION, RHYTHM, AND COMBINATION OF THE FOUR.

CHAPTER 42
THE HUNGARIAN MINOR SCALE
FORMULA: W H WH H H WH H
APPLIED TO C

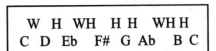

W	H	WH	H	H	WH	H
C	D	Eb	F#	G	Ab	B	C

KEY OF C HUNGARIAN MINOR

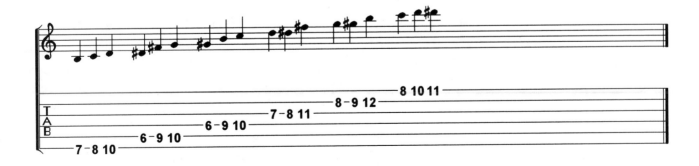

NOW APPLY THIS SCALE TO EVERY KEY, TECHNIQUE, APPLICATION, RHYTHM, AND COMBINATION OF THE FOUR.

CHAPTER 43
THE JAPANESE SCALE
FORMULA: W WH H WH WH
APPLIED TO C

W	WH	H	WH	WH
C	D	F G	A	C

KEY OF C JAPANESE

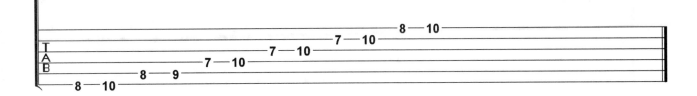

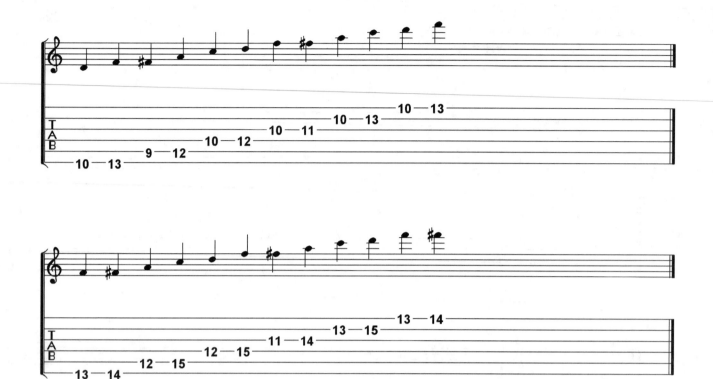

NOW APPLY THIS SCALE TO EVERY KEY, TECHNIQUE, APPLICATION, RHYTHM, AND COMBINATION OF THE FOUR.

CHAPTER 44
THE JAPANESE b2 SCALE
FORMULA: H WW H WH WH
APPLIED TO C

H	WW	H	WH	WH
C	Db	F	Gb	A	C

KEY OF C JAPANESE b2

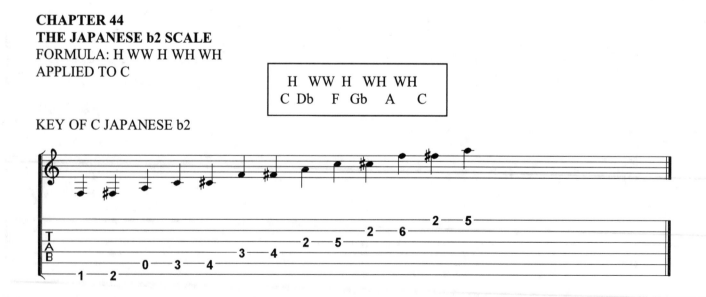

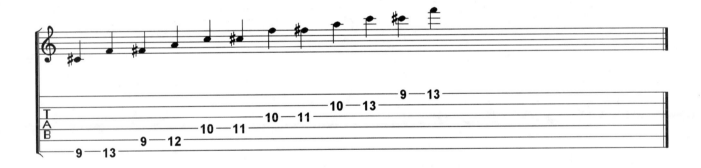

NOW APPLY THIS SCALE TO EVERY KEY, TECHNIQUE, APPLICATION, RHYTHM, AND COMBINATION OF THE FOUR.

CHAPTER 45
THE MAJOR 7, #5 SCALE
FORMULA: W W H WH H W H
APPLIED TO C

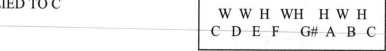

W	W	H	WH	H	W	H
C	D	E	F	G#	A	B	C

KEY OF C MAJOR 7, #5

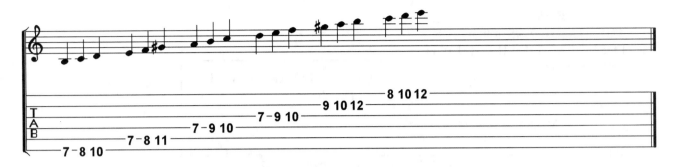

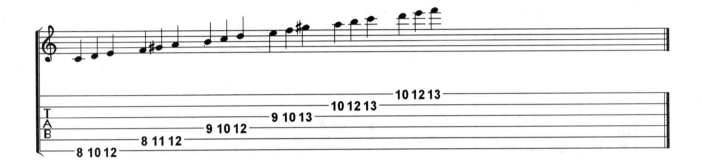

NOW APPLY THIS SCALE TO EVERY KEY, TECHNIQUE, APPLICATION, RHYTHM, AND COMBINATION OF THE FOUR.

CHAPTER 46
THE MAJOR 7, #5, # 9 SCALE
FORMULA: WH H H WH H W H
APPLIED TO C

WH		H	H	WH		H	W	H
C	D#		E	F	G#		A	B	C

KEY OF C MAJOR 7, #5, #9

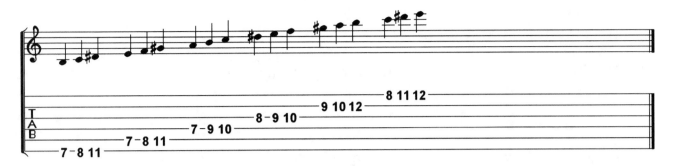

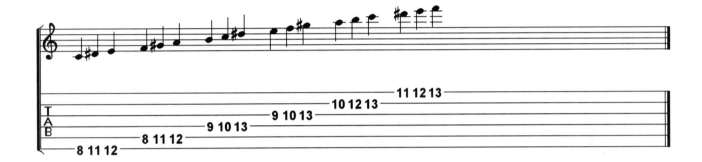

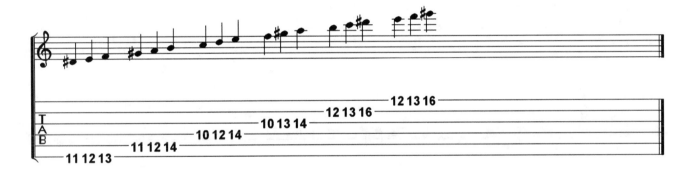

NOW APPLY THIS SCALE TO EVERY KEY, TECHNIQUE, APPLICATION, RHYTHM, AND COMBINATION OF THE FOUR.

CHAPTER 47
THE MELODIC MINOR SCALE
FORMULA: W H W W W W H
APPLIED TO C

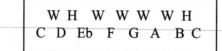

W	H	W	W	W	W	H
C	D	Eb	F	G	A	B	C

KEY OF C MELODIC MINOR

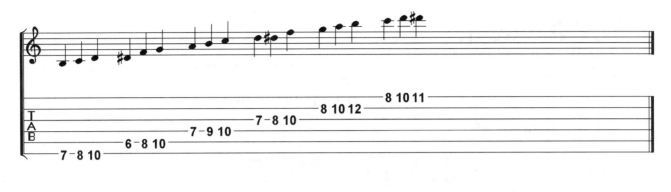

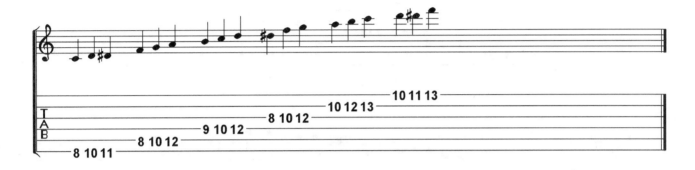

CLASSICAL THEORY: Composers of classical music often use the Melodic Minor scale ascending, then use the natural minor scale of the same key to descend as in the example below.

Melodic Minor Ascending   Natural Minor Descending

CHAPTER 48
THE MINOR 7, b5 SCALE
FORMULA: W H W H WH H W
APPLIED TO C

W	H	W	H	WH	H	W	
C	D	Eb	F	Gb	A	Bb	C

KEY OF C MINOR 7, b5

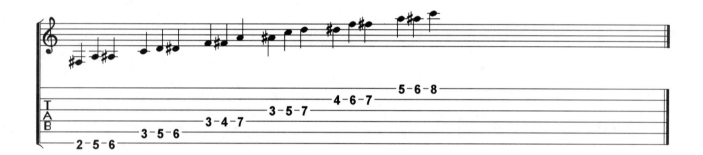

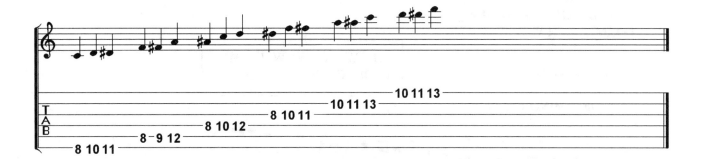

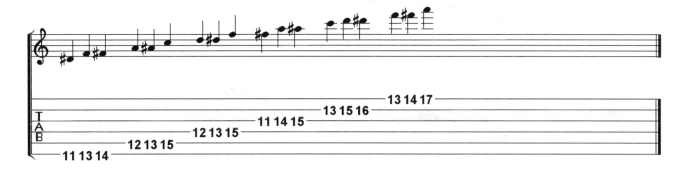

NOW APPLY THIS SCALE TO EVERY KEY, TECHNIQUE, APPLICATION, RHYTHM, AND COMBINATION OF THE FOUR.

CHAPTER 49
THE MINOR 7, b9 SCALE
FORMULA: H W W W W H W

H	W	W	W	W	H	W
C	Db	Eb	F	G	A	Bb	C

APPLIED TO C

KEY OF C MINOR 7, b9

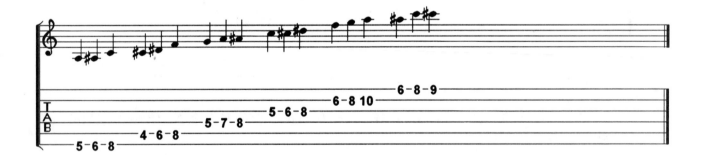

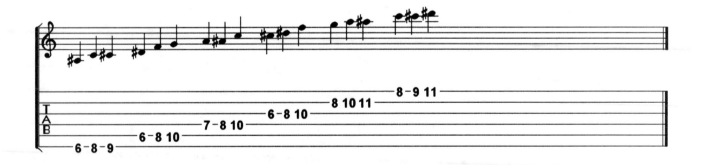

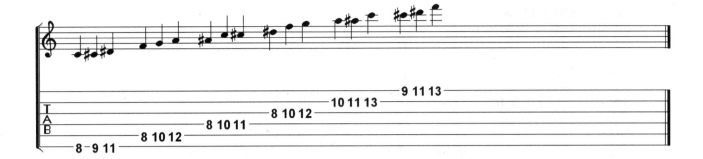

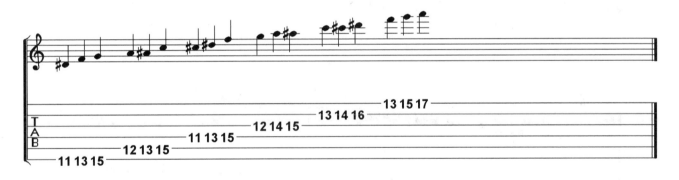

NOW APPLY THIS SCALE TO EVERY KEY, TECHNIQUE, APPLICATION, RHYTHM, AND COMBINATION OF THE FOUR.

CHAPTER 50
THE MINOR 7, b5, b9 SCALE
FORMULA: H W W H WH H W
APPLIED TO C

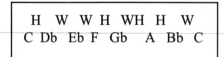

H	W	W	H	WH	H	W
C	Db	Eb	F	Gb	A	Bb	C

KEY OF C MINOR 7, b5, b9

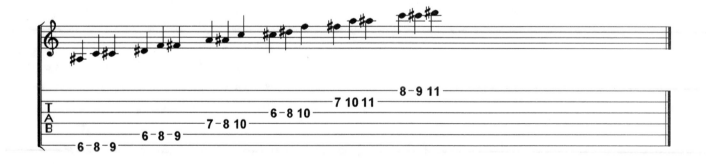

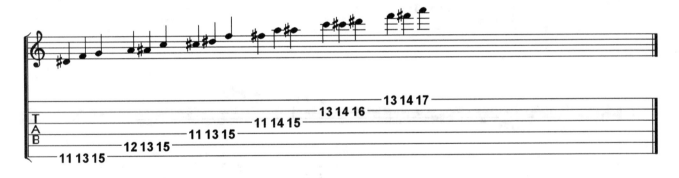

NOW APPLY THIS SCALE TO EVERY KEY, TECHNIQUE, APPLICATION, RHYTHM, AND COMBINATION OF THE FOUR.

CHAPTER 51
THE NEAPOLITAN SCALE
FORMULA: H W W W H WH H
APPLIED TO C

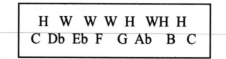

H	W	W	W	H	WH	H	
C	Db	Eb	F	G	Ab	B	C

KEY OF C NEAPOLITAN

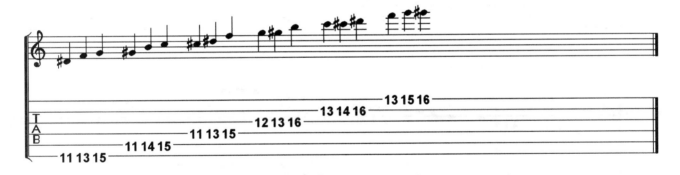

NOW APPLY THIS SCALE TO EVERY KEY, TECHNIQUE, APPLICATION, RHYTHM, AND COMBINATION OF THE FOUR.

CHAPTER 52
THE NEAPOLITAN MINOR SCALE
FORMULA: H W W W W W H
APPLIED TO C

H	W	W	W	W	W	H
C	Db	Eb	F	G	A	B	C

KEY OF C NEAPOLITAN MINOR SCALE

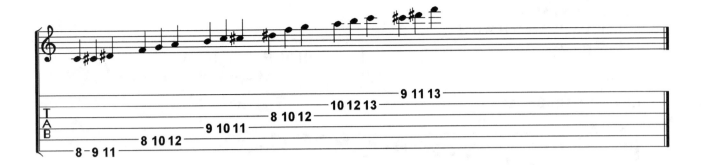

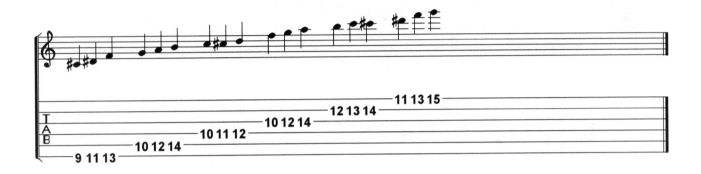

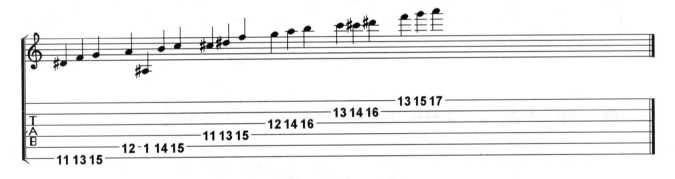

NOW APPLY THIS SCALE TO EVERY KEY, TECHNIQUE, APPLICATION, RHYTHM, AND COMBINATION OF THE FOUR.

CHAPTER 53
THE ORIENTAL SCALE
FORMULA: H WH H H WH H W
APPLIED TO C

H	WH	H	H	WH	H	W
C	Db	E	F	Gb	A	Bb	C

KEY OF C ORIENTAL

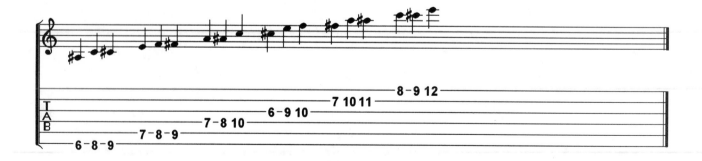

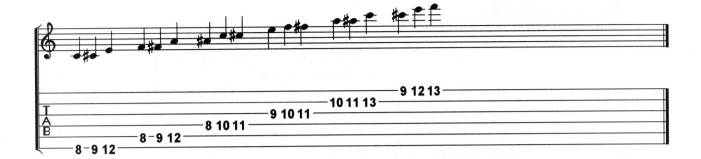

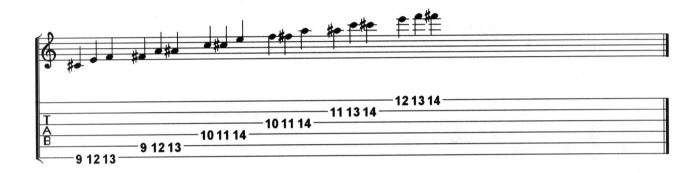

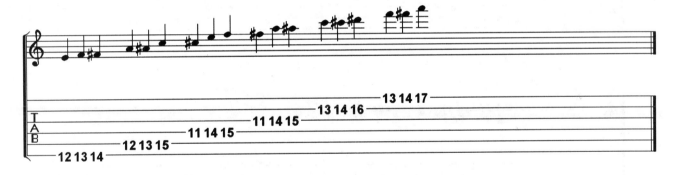

NOW APPLY THIS SCALE TO EVERY KEY, TECHNIQUE, APPLICATION, RHYTHM, AND COMBINATION OF THE FOUR.

CHAPTER 54
THE PERSIAN SCALE
FORMULA: H WH H H W WH H
APPLIED TO C

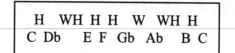

H	WH	H H	W	WH H
C Db		E F	Gb	Ab	B C

KEY OF C PERSIAN

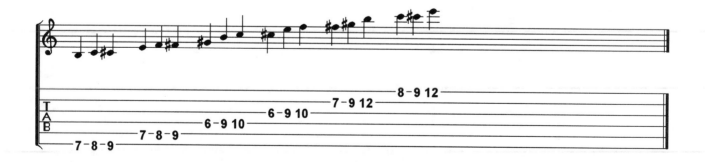

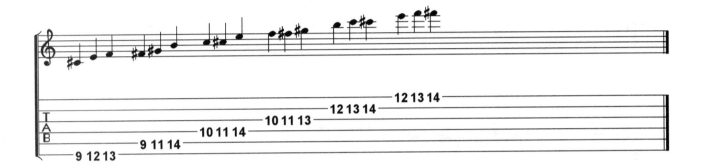

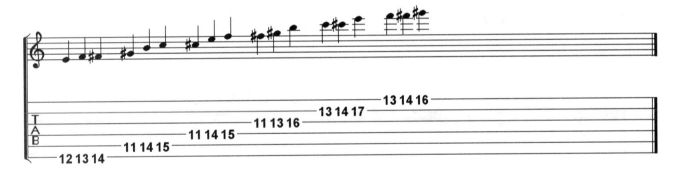

NOW APPLY THIS SCALE TO EVERY KEY, TECHNIQUE, APPLICATION, RHYTHM, AND COMBINATION OF THE FOUR.

CHAPTER 55
THE SPANISH SCALE
FORMULA: H W H H H W W W

APPLIED TO C

KEY OF C SPANISH

H	W	H	H	H	W	W	W
C	Db	Eb	E	F	Gb	Ab	Bb	C

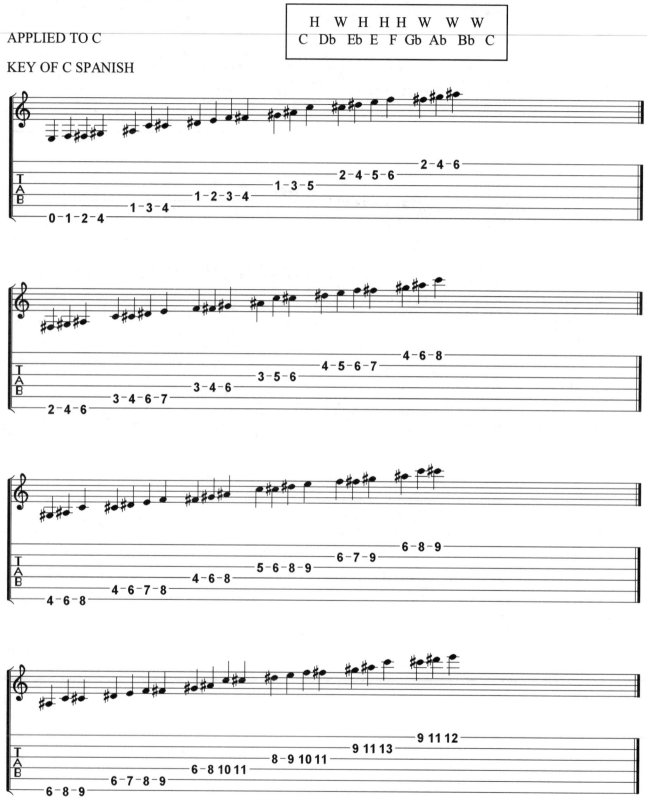

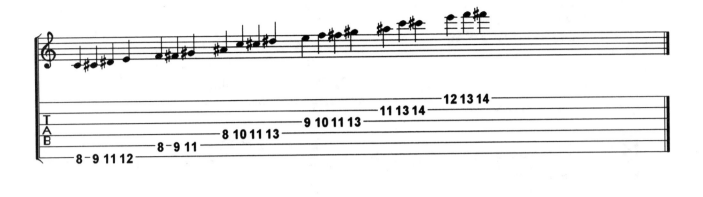

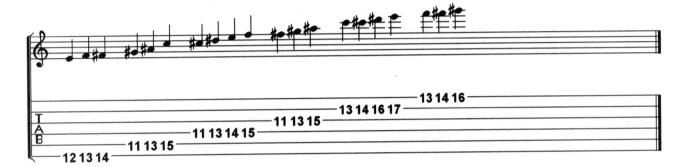

NOW APPLY THIS SCALE TO EVERY KEY, TECHNIQUE, APPLICATION, RHYTHM, AND COMBINATION OF THE FOUR.

CHAPTER 56
THE SPANISH GYPSY SCALE
FORMULA: H WH H W H W W
APPLIED TO C

H	WH	H	W	H	W	W
C	Db	E	F	G	Ab	Bb	C

KEY OF C SPANISH GYPSY

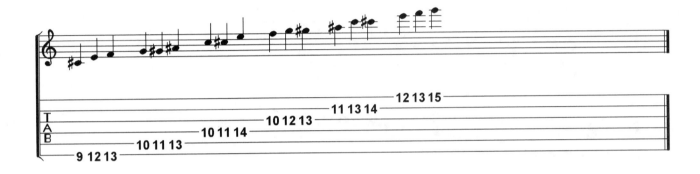

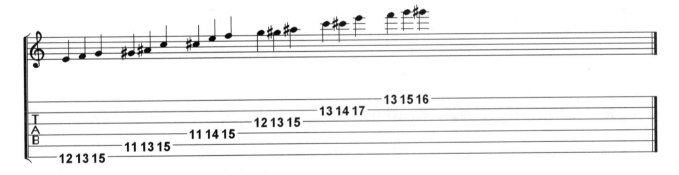

NOW APPLY THIS SCALE TO EVERY KEY, TECHNIQUE, APPLICATION, RHYTHM, AND COMBINATION OF THE FOUR.

CHAPTER 57
THE WHOLE TONE SCALE
FORMULA: W W W W W W

APPLIED TO C

W	W	W	W	W	W
C	D	E	F#	G#	A#	C

KEY OF C WHOLE TONE SCALE

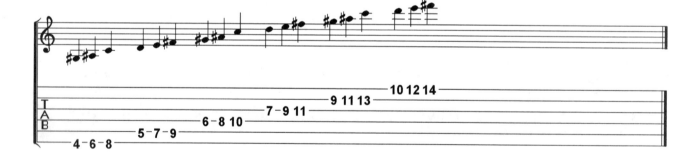

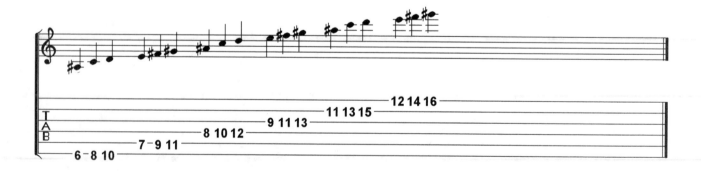

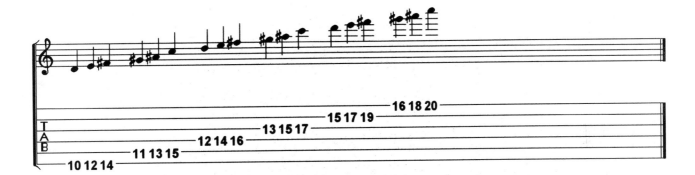

NOW APPLY THIS SCALE TO EVERY KEY, TECHNIQUE, APPLICATION, RHYTHM, AND COMBINATION OF THE FOUR.

CHAPTER 58
THE CHROMATIC SCALE
FORMULA: H H H H H H H H H H H H

H	H	H		H	H	H		H	H		H	H	
C	C#	D	D#	E	F	F#	G	G#	A	A#	B	C	

CHROMATIC SCALE

NOW APPLY THIS SCALE TO EVERY KEY, TECHNIQUE, APPLICATION, RHYTHM, AND
COMBINATION OF THE FOUR.

2008 CLOSING STATEMENTS

This method began as a bundle of papers which I used to organize my concept of playing the guitar. It dates as far back as the 1980's and continues to evolve even to this day.

In the first half of the 1990s I began teaching at The Music Mart in Largo, Florida. I would grab a sheet from my bundle that catered to a student's level, photocopy it, and we would work on the material. Some time between 1994 to 1996 I organized these notes into a binder and sold them as a text book to my private students. The original price was $40, plus tuition.

In the late summer of 1996 a man entered The Music Mart and asked to speak to me. He said he was a friend of one of my private students. He had seen my lesson binder and he wanted to purchase a copy but he did not want to take lessons. I initially told him the text was only available to private students. He reasoned that if I didn't sell him a copy he could easily borrow it from his friend, or even make a photocopy. I quickly reconsidered and made the sale.

It was that transaction which inspired me to write a book based on my method. Since the student version had only hand written sheet music, tab and charts (there was no text at all), I now had the task of writing descriptions to go along with each exercise. Being unhappy with the other guitar instruction books on the market, I wanted to make sure mine was different. Most methods from that era only gave a small amount of information. That way you would have to buy book 2 or book 3 if you wanted to learn more on the subject. Others were too technical for a beginner to understand, and some were completely vague. My book would have to be descriptive and progressive to insure that a guitarist of any level, beginner through professional, would be able to comprehend what I was teaching.

As I set out to write the first edition I could not afford the expensive music software that was available so I used a basic word program. The original version of TSTA was only available in Tablature. Just TAB! No staff. No notation. Not even notes for timing reference. The lessons in the "vintage" version of TSTA looked like this:

```
TECH/APP COMBO
HAMMER ONS AND THREE STRINGS                                           h  h
-------------------------------------------------------------h--h-----------------h--h----8-10-12--
-----------------------------------------------h-h-----------------h-h----8-10-12---h--h---8-10-12------------
-------------------h-h----------------h-h---7-9-10-----h-h----7-9-10------------7-9-10--------------------
----------h-h---7-9-10----h-h---7-9-10-----------7-9-10--------------------------------------
--h-h---7-8-10-----------7-8-10------------------------------------------------------------------
-7-8-10-----------------------------------------------------------------------------------
 1 &  a  2 & a   3 & a    etc...
```

I did all the programing myself, each tab line dot ----, each number, spacing, symbol, etc., all on a standard computer word program. Despite its primitive presentation, the book still sold well and paved the way for several reprints.

First Printing April 1, 1998

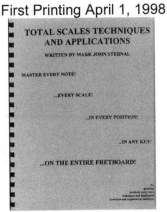

The original cover was printed on green cardboard stock, and spiral bound at a PIP Printing store in Clearwater, FL. The text was 67 pages long.

Although my wife Jeanne and I focused mainly on our retail business selling musical instruments and teaching music, it was obvious that TSTA was a successful self-published title. In 2001, after selling several thousand copies of the spiral bound edition, we decided to have the book printed in magazine format with a staple bound color cover. The text was now 68 pages.

2001 Staple Bound Edition

The staple bound version sold an additional 10,000 copies from June 2001 to April of 2004. This number could have been much higher but we did not have distribution through book or music stores. All 10,000 copies were sold direct via mail order. Most were sold on eBay or other online auction websites. Catapulted by eBay's feedback feature, TSTA unarguably became the best selling guitar method on eBay. In fact, largely due to sales of TSTA, Jeanne and I became one of eBay's top 200 sellers in the electronics/musical instrument category (screen name wriverroad).

As our stock of the staple bound version became depleted, we discussed taking the next step to begin a licensed publishing company to get our titles distributed through stores. This meant rewriting TSTA with traditional notation in addition to TAB. The 2004 edition now had more than double the pages and a perfect bound (paperback) full color cover. The cover images were licensed and endorsed by Gibson Guitars and featured my 1993 Les Paul electric and 2001 J-150 acoustic guitars (Gibson would later endorse the DVD version as well).

In 2005 the book was enhanced by the inclusion of a CD with me performing all of the exercises, giving the reader a practical reference of what each scale, technique and application should sound like.

I was once told that a "good" book isn't written. It is written, then re-written, re-written and re-written. I *have* officially lost count of how many times I have revised and added to the TSTA method. Each time the book was ready for a reprint I found something to add. Today I've completed the revised 2008 version, making this the most complete version of GUITAR: Total Scales Techniques and Applications to date.

As Always: Life, Love and Music,
Mark John Sternal
May 14, 2008

E-mail Mark at msternal@mjspublications.com

BONUS MATERIAL

BONUS MODE CHARTS

As a bonus, I've added a Master Mode Chart combining all seven modes. The fingerings are the same, but initials for each mode, or rather mode root, have been added to the note charts. For more on Modes see pages 89 and 102.

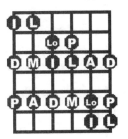
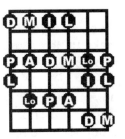

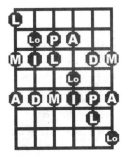

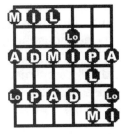
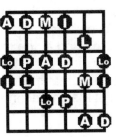
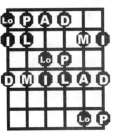

I = Ionian, D = Dorian, P = Phrygian, L = Lydian, M = Mixolydian, A = Aeolian, Lo = Locrian

ADVANCED LEAD GUITAR CONCEPTS

Playing Over Major Chords

Major: The most obvious scale to use is major.

Example: If you are playing over a C major chord use the C major scale.

Minor: You can offer some contrast to the progression by focusing on the relative minor root note.

Example: In the key of C major, the A note is the relative minor.

Pentatonic: Major pentatonic and/or minor pentatonic both work well with over major chords.

Alternative Keys: The major scale of the 4th and 5th scale degrees of the root of your chord can be played as alternative scales.

Example: In the key of C, the 4th scale degree if F and the 5th scale degree is G. The F major scale and G major scale both consist of the notes C-E-G which make up the C major chord.

Modes: Ionian (same as major), Lydian and Mixolydian all work because they share the same notes that make up the major chord.

Example: If you are playing over a C major chord, the C Ionian, Lydian and Mixolydian modes share the same notes that make up the C chord (root=C, major third=E, fifth=G).

Contrasting Modes: Dorian, Phrygian and Aeolian will work in some cases because they share the root and fifth, but they include a minor third (Eb) which will contrast with the major third (E) played by the rhythm guitar.

Example: The C major chord is made up of C-E-G. These modes share the C and G note, but include Eb instead of E.

Finally, the Locrian mode can be played for a strong contrast. The only common tone is the root note, the third and fifth scale tones are both flat.

Exotic Scales: Any scale consisting of notes that make up your chord will compliment the chord. In some cases you may only need some of the chord tones present to use an exotic scale, but this will ultimately depend on your taste.

Playing Over Minor Chords

Minor: The most obvious scale to use is minor.

Example: If you are playing over an A minor chord use the A minor scale.

Major: You can offer some contrast to the progression by focusing on the relative major root note.

Example: In the key of A minor, the C note is the relative major.

Pentatonic: Minor pentatonic works best with minor chords.

Alternative Keys: You can also play the major scales of the 6th and 7th scale degree of your minor chord.

Example: In A minor, the 6th scale degree is F and the 7th scale degree is G. The F major scale and G major scale both consist of the notes A-C-E which make up the A minor chord.

Modes: The Dorian, Phrygian and Aeolian (same as minor) all work because they share the notes that make up the minor chord.

Example: If you are playing over an A minor chord, the A Dorian, Phrygian and Aeolian modes share the same notes that make up the A minor chord (root=A, minor third=C, fifth=E).

Contrasting Modes: The Locrian mode can be played, but will have a contrast if you focus on the flat 5th over the minor chord (which is played with a 5th).

The Ionian, Lydian and Mixolydian modes will work in some cases because they share the same root and fifth as the chord being played. The contrasting notes are the major thirds in these modes, which do not blend well with the minor 3rd used in the minor chord. In most cases it will work as an effect, but not through an entire song.

Exotic Scales: Any scale consisting of notes that make up your chord will compliment the chord. In some cases you may only need some of the chord tones present to use an exotic scale, but this will ultimately depend on your taste.

Playing Over Progressions or Songs

The previous lead guitar formulas give examples for playing over a chord type. When you look at a progression or song as a whole, your options change drastically. Here are some example formulas for playing over common progressions in the key of C.

Playing Over 2 Chord Progressions: C F (I IV)

Major: The most obvious scale to use is C major.

Minor: You can offer some contrast to the progression by focusing on A, the relative minor root note.

Pentatonic: C major pentatonic and/or C minor pentatonic both work well with this progression.

Alternative Keys: The Key of F shares all of the notes used by both chords in this progression, C-E-G for the C chord and F-A-C for the F chord.

Changing With The Chords: You can also play the F Major and G Major scales over the C chord because both consist of the notes C, E & G which make up the C major chord. When the progression changes to the F chord you can play the Bb scale in addition to the C or F scale, all of which use the notes F-A-C which make up the F chord.

Modes: C Ionian (same as major) and Mixolydian both work because they share the same notes as the C and F chords (C-E-G, and F-A-C).

Contrasting Modes: The C Lydian mode will work in some cases because it has all the notes of the C chord (C-E-G). The F chord (F-A-C) will have a contrast with this mode since it uses a F#. This mode would work best when played over the C, but switch to a more compatible mode when the progression changes from C to the F chord.

The C Dorian will work in some cases because it has all the notes of the F chord (F-A-C), but only the root and 5th of the C chord, the Eb scale note contrasts with the E played in the C chord.

C Phrygian and Aeolian will work in some cases because they share the root and fifth of both the C and F chords, but they include the minor third of both chords which will contrast with the major third played by the rhythm guitar.

The Locrian mode can be played for a strong contrast. The only common tone with the C chord is the root note, the third and fifth scale tones are both flat, Eb and Gb. This mode does share the root and 5th of the F chord, but the third is flat (Ab).

While playing along with the CD, you might find that these modes work better when you pan your speakers to just drums and bass.

Exotic Scales: Any scale consisting of notes C, E, F, G & A will compliment this progression. In some cases you may only need some of the chord tones present to use an exotic scale, but this will ultimately depend on your taste.

Playing Over 3 Chord Progressions: C F G (I IV V)

Major: The most obvious scale to use is C major since all of the chords (and their notes) are within the C major scale.

Minor: You can offer some contrast to the progression by focusing on A, the relative minor root note.

Pentatonic: C major pentatonic will work best for a Country feel. Changing to C minor pentatonic will add a Blues flavor to the mix.

Changing With The Chords: You can also play the F Major and G Major scales over the C chord because both consist of the notes C, E & G which make up the C major chord. When the progression changes to the F chord you can play the Bb scale in addition to the C or F scale, all of which use the notes F-A-C which make up the F chord. When changing to the G chord you can play the G, D and C major scales, which consist of the notes G-B-D found in the G chord.

Modes: C Ionian (same as major) share the same 7 notes which make up the three chords in this progression.

Contrasting Modes: C Mixolydian will work over the C and F chords, but will have a contrast when played over G because of the Bb in the scale. This mode would work best when played over the C and F, but you might want to switch to a more compatible mode when the progression changes to the G chord.

The C Lydian mode will work over the C and G chord because they share the same notes. The F chord (F-A-C) will have a contrast with this mode since it uses a F#. This mode would work best when played over the C and G, but you might want to switch to a more compatible mode when the progression changes to the F chord.

The C Dorian will work in some cases because it has all the notes of the F chord (F-A-C), but only the root and 5th of the C and G chords, the Eb scale note contrasts with the E played in the C chord, and the Bb scale note will contrast with the B played in the G chord.

C Aeolian will work in some cases because it shares the root and fifth of all 3 chords, but it includes the minor third of each chord which will contrast with the major third played by the rhythm guitar.

C Phrygian will work in some cases because it shares the root and fifth of both the C and F chords, but they include the minor third of both chords which will contrast with the major third played by the rhythm guitar. This mode will strongly contrast with the G chord (G-B-D) since the only note in common is G, the contrasting notes are Bb and Db.

The Locrian mode can be played for a strong contrast. The only common tone with the C chord is the root note, the third and fifth scale tones are both flat, Eb and Gb. This mode does share the root and 5th of the F chord, but the third is flat (Ab). The C Locrian mode does not have any common notes with the G chord.

Exotic Scales: Any scale consisting of notes C, D, E, F, G, A & B will compliment this progression. In some cases you may only need some of the chord tones present to use an exotic scale, but this will ultimately depend on your taste.

Join The TSTA Lead Guitar Forum

These are just a few examples. There are countless more scenarios and possibilities. For more ideas about playing lead guitar over different chords and progressions please visit the MJS TSTA Lead Guitar Forum. There you can share your ideas, questions and comments for using scales, modes, techniques and melody applications when playing along with other musicians or over common chord progressions. Visit http://forums.mjspublications.com/

Get TSTA updates at http://www.mjspublications.com/moretsta.php

ALSO AVAILABLE FROM MJS MUSIC & ENTERTAINMENT

NOW ON DVD!

GUITAR DVD: Total Scales Techniques and Applications

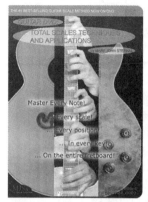

This complete course starts with a bonus beginner section to insure that any guitarist at any level can use this video. It quickly progresses to intermediate –then advanced levels of playing.

First begin with universal shapes found in every key of music to expertly play scales and leads on the entire fretboard. Don't worry about memorizing these positions! Memory will come naturally when Mark John Sternal demonstrates how to use these scales musically. Tasty licks, tricks and techniques like hammer ons, pull offs, picking patterns, vibrato, string bending, two hand tapping. Plus techniques exclusive to electric guitar including tremolo bar, string bending, and electronic control tricks. In addition you'll learn a ton of applications to make your lead guitar and melody lines stand out, and make learning your favorite songs a breeze: increment patterns, string skipping, double note patterns (harmony), two handed tapping, harmonics. All of this and more is introduced in a song context, giving thorough examples of how these scales, techniques and applications can be used with chords and song structure.

To wrap up this amazing instructional DVD, Mark teaches you all of the modes, key changes, plus 50 exotic and cultural scales –all on the entire fretboard!

You'll be amazed at how expertly Mark John Sternal has simplified the art of understanding and using the guitar fretboard.

GTSTA DVD - 89192600200 - ONLY $24.95

BASS GUITAR: Total Scales Techniques and Applications

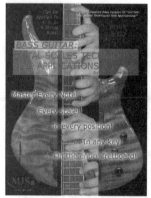

The First and only method to expertly teach you every scale, every trick & technique, in every musical key, anywhere on the entire fretboard! Author Mark John Sternal has been credited as one of the greatest music instructors of the 21st Century! His credentials accumulate to thousands of beginner through advanced bass players and guitarists. This course promises to turn beginners into pro's & make the pro's even better!

BTSTA - Book & CD - ISBN-13: 978-0976291756 - ONLY $24.95

GUITARRA: Escalas, Técnicas y Aplicaciones Totales

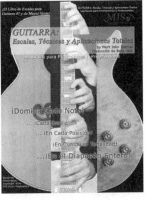

Recomendado para cualquier guitarrista, sin importar su habilidad o gusto musicales. Comienza con todas las bases necesarias para un principiante, pero va avanzando a un paso constante a través de técnicas y aplicaciones avanzadas y profesionales.

Una enciclopedia de escalas, pero aún más que eso, este método te enseña cómo usar estas escalas para hacer música.

Éste es el único curso que vas a necesitar para aprender a tocar escalas y tocar guitara líder. ¡Todo en un solo libro!

SPTSTA - Book - ISBN-13: 978-0976291756 - ONLY $14.95

Easy Guitar Chords DVD
Common Rhythms and Progressions

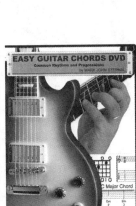

Chords are the canvas for any song in any style of music. Using only 3 or 4 chords, guitarists can entertain their audience for hours! From a single player at a campfire, or an afternoon on the front porch with friends and family, to an open blues jam, folk festival or stadium rock concert –You are guaranteed to find one similarity: CHORDS! This video course includes easy, basic chords found in every key of music –presented in a useful format showing you how chords and chord combinations are used musically. By introducing rhythms and chord progressions, each section progresses to be more than just a handful of chords ...you will actually learn to play and make music with guitar chords!

Every chord, rhythm and progression is introduced with a thorough on-screen demonstration, followed by an example played with a tempo. The bottom half of the screen provides you with the option of reading chord charts, traditional notation, or tablature (TAB). As a bonus, you also get important tips for spicing up chords by the use of strumming patterns, finger picking, raking and rests. There is also a still-image section detailing the sheet music and chord progressions found throughout the video. A built in tuner will help keep your guitar in tune, and on screen metronomes allow you to practice chords and rhythm progressions at several different speeds.

EZGChords - DVD - 891926002038 - Only $12.95

EASY GUITAR SCALES DVD
Over 50 Common and Exotic Scales and Modes For Guitar

Scales are the foundation of music and can be found in every known culture. With all styles of modern music, scales are the heartbeat, breath and soul of the guitar solo, the guitar riff and even the vocal melody! This video course includes every guitar scale you've ever wanted to learn - presented in a simple root to octave format, starting with basic scales, such as major, minor, pentatonic and blues, and then progressing into patterns that span all musical styles and cultures, even including exotic scales such as the Balinese, Hirojoshi and Kumoi.

There are over 50 scales for you to use right away to spice up your guitar playing, each with an on-screen demonstration at both a slow and fast tempo. The bottom half of the screen provides you with the option of reading sheet music in the form of note charts, traditional notation, or tablature (TAB). As a bonus, you also get important tips on changing musical keys, jumping octaves and extending each scale to a higher and lower pitch, which will ultimately help you navigate your fretboard with precision and accuracy.

EZGScales - DVD - 891926002021 - Only $12.95

GUITAR DVD #1
Beginner Basics and Beyond

For electric or acoustic, this video gives you all you need to survive in the world of guitar! Designed to be the FASTEST and EASIEST way to learn to play, GUARANTEED! Learn to read guitar music with notation, TAB and charts. Start playing instantly! Learn individual notes then progressively build up to partial and full chords. Graduate to your first 5 SONGS in the most popular music styles including Rock, Blues and Country.

BONUS FEATURES: Built in metronome and guitar tuner. Giant on-screen sheet music. The guitars and amps of GUITAR DVD #1. Over 3 Jam Packed Hours!

GDVD1 - DVD - 891926002014 - Only $14.95

GUITAR: Probable Chords
a "Chord Key Encyclopedia"

In this volume Mark John Sternal sets out to achieve what no other music instruction publisher has ever accomplished. The expert reviews, along with thousands of raving customer testimonies are indication that he has surpassed his goal with GUITAR: Probable Chords.

The unique name comes from the investigative term Probable Cause, and like a crime scene investigator, Mark digs deep into the world of guitar chords. In this one of a kind chord method he teaches you to use every chord, from basic structures to intermediate and advanced extensions and variations -in every key of music, and how to use them to write and play songs.

288 page book with narration/performance audio CD, complete course for beginner through advanced.

GPC - Book & CD - ISBN-13: 978-0976291763 - ONLY $24.95

COMPLETE GUITAR BY EAR:

2 CD Relative Pitch Ear Training Course –LEARN EVERY NOTE ON YOUR GUITAR COMPLETELY BY EAR! No written text or sheet music. Over 50 recorded lessons. A proven system that will help you develop a strong musical ear, finger strength, and an understanding of music theory for guitar. Just pop in the CDs and follow the lessons from your very first note to every note -on every fret -on every string of your guitar.

2 CDs Total running time: 1 hour 41 minutes

CGE - Audiobook on CD - ISBN-13: 978-0976291732 - ONLY $22.95

COMPLETE BASS GUITAR BY EAR:
2 CD Relative Pitch Ear Training Course

LEARN EVERY NOTE ON YOUR BASS GUITAR COMPLETELY BY EAR! No written text or sheet music. Over 50 recorded lessons. A proven system that will help you develop a strong musical ear, finger strength, and an understanding of music theory for bass guitar. Just pop in the CDs and follow the lessons from your very first note to every note -on every fret -on every string of your guitar.

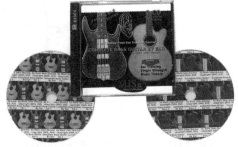

2 CDs Total running time: 1 hour 40 minutes

CBGE - Audiobook on CD - ISBN-13: 978-0976291749 - ONLY $22.95

THE TWELVE NOTES OF MUSIC:
Music Theory Simplified

There are only 12 notes in the musical alphabet, when you have mastered them you have mastered music. Take an in depth look at each individual note and learn how it associates with other notes, giving you a full understanding of the tonal structure of melodies, harmonies, and chords.

Whether you are a beginner or an advanced musician you will gain a world of insight by learning our twelve musical tones!

–24 Page Study Course
–Improve pitch recognition and note relativity
–Start with one note and build at your own pace
–Written with charts and thoroughly explained instructions
–No sheet music or sight reading necessary
–Each chapter is built on what you have previously learned
–Learn to easily build any scale or chord structure

12N - Book - ISBN-13: 978-0976291725 - ONLY $7.95

To Order Additional Copies Of This Book
Or To Order Other Titles From MJS Music & Entertainment

Online www.mjspublications.com
Toll Free Order Line: 1-866-463-9247
For Customer Service: 1-352-563-1779
Mail Orders:
MJS Music & Entertainment, LLC
9699 W. Fort Island Trail
Crystal River, FL 34429

GUITAR: Total Scales Techniques and Applications (BOOK & CD)
GTSTA Quantity _____ x $24.95 ea.

GUITAR DVD: Total Scales Techniques and Applications
GTSTA DVD Quantity _____ x $24.95 ea.

GUITAR COMBO Total Scales Techniques Applications (DVD/Book/CD)
GTSTA COMBO Quantity _____ x $39.95 ea.

BASS GUITAR: Total Scales Techniques and Applications (BOOK & CD)
BTSTA Quantity _____ x $24.95 ea.

GUITARRA: Escalas, Técnicas y Aplicaciones Totales (Book Only)
SPTSTA Quantity _____ x $14.95 ea.

EASY GUITAR CHORDS DVD
EZGChords _____ x $12.95

EASY GUITAR SCALES DVD
EZGScales _____ x $12.95

GUITAR DVD #1 Beginner Basics & Beyond
GDVD1 _____ x $14.95

GUITAR: Probable Chords (BOOK & CD)
GPC Quantity _____ x $24.95

COMPLETE GUITAR BY EAR
CGE Quantity _____ x $22.95

COMPLETE BASS GUITAR BY EAR
CBGE Quantity _____ x $22.95

THE TWELVE NOTES OF MUSIC
12N Quantity _____ x $7.95

SHIPPING: Add $3.95 for any title, plus $2.00 for each additional title for shipping in the USA.
Florida residents add 6% sales tax.

NOTES

ABOUT THE AUTHOR

Musician, Educator and Author Mark John Sternal began teaching his trademark method to private guitar students in 1991. He was only 17, with one year left of High School before he would attend Richard Daley College in Chicago. By 1994 Mark relocated to Florida, and with him came the manuscript of his first book. The piece was titled Total Scales Techniques and Applications, which Mark sold to his private students. One afternoon a student's friend came into the music store where Mark was teaching. He explained that he had seen the manuscript and wanted to purchase one for himself. This transaction sparked the idea to put the manuscript up for sale online. The manuscript sold so well that Mark was able to quit his "other job" as a student loan consultant, and pursue music full time. By 2002, fueled by user feedback and testimonials, Mark's growing number of music instruction titles awarded him national recognition. In 2004 his proven methods became available to the retail music industry. For most of 2006 and all of 2007 MJS held the #1 best selling music instruction slot at some of the largest music and book stores in the United States. In Late 2007 Mark released the long awaited GUITAR DVD: Total Scales Techniques and Applications. Scheduled for release during the first half of 2008 is GUITAR DVD #1 Beginner Basics & Beyond, GUITAR: Total Scales Techniques and Applications 2008 Revised Edition, Easy Guitar Scales DVD and Easy Guitar Chords DVD, all written and performed by Mark John Sternal.

When he isn't traveling and performing throughout the United States, Mark John Sternal performs regularly in his home town of Crystal River, FL. Mark performs acoustic guitar solo and duo shows, and electric guitar with a 3 to 5 piece band.

MJS
Music & Entertainment

www.mjspublications.com